I am so glad Joel is finally puttin
of the grace and power of God.   ...for many years and have
so much respect for his passion to see people live out their lives for God's
fame. You will soon read in The Father I Never Had that Joel understands
life doesn't play fair. But we are sons and daughters of a perfect Father and
He holds us all together.

Chris Tomlin
Dove Award Winning Recording Artist, Six-Steps Records

The Father I Never Had is one of those books that you will read voraciously
due to the story of redemption...but will come back to time and again as a
resource and tool for ministry in your own life as well as for use in ministry
to others. Joel has known abandonment, rejection, and the subsequent anger,
disillusionment, and shame that go hand in hand with sin - even as a believer
in and follower of Jesus Christ...yet he has found what we all are indeed
looking for. THE Answer. To know a father's love - THE Father's love - and to
BE KNOWN is the deepest desire of every human existence. Do you desire to
know Him and to be known by Him more deeply than you thought possible?
Read The Father I Never Had.

Dennis Jernigan
Worship Leader, Author, Song Receiver
More importantly: Husband to Melinda and Father of Nine Most Cherished Blessings

The Father I Never Had is a powerful story that will have you gripped
from the first page to the last. Joel Engle uses his life journey to draw the
reader in, knowing that the redemptive truth in these pages will change
lives for God's glory. Read it, and you'll never be the same...

David Nasser
Author of "A Call To Die", International Communicator, David Nasser Outreach

THE FATHER I NEVER HAD

THE FATHER I NEVER HAD

JOEL ENGLE

FOREWORD BY STAN MOSER

LUCIDBOOKS

THE FATHER I NEVER HAD

FOREWORD

" . . . For the LORD does not see as man sees;
for man looks at the outward appearance,
but the LORD looks at the heart."
1 Samuel 16:7

W hen I first met Joel Engle, he certainly didn't look like a pastor. In fact, he looked exactly like what he was—a self-made Christian songwriter and recording artist.

At that time, I had been an executive in the Christian music industry for over thirty years. During our meeting, Joel reminded me that we had considered signing him as an artist for our StarSong record label just a few years earlier. I probably pretended to remember, but honestly, he was one of many musicians who made the "rejection list" over the years.

I had no way of knowing just how many times Joel had been on the rejection list in other parts of his life, but I would soon find out. You see, this was not a chance meeting. It was a divine appointment for two men destined to become friends, partners, and co-laborers for Christ.

I must admit that the music Joel played for me in my office that day was very good. But his attitude really wasn't. He just didn't trust anyone connected with Nashville's Christian music scene. And before long, I understood why.

Many years earlier in a city two time zones away, a young boy named Joel was born into a world that would soon be filled with rejection. It started with a father who never showed up and a mother who left unable to say goodbye. Rejection by a Nashville record label paled in comparison.

Yet, young Joel had pressed on through life. In spite of the overwhelming losses as a child, the teenage Joel discovered the musical talent and gifts that God had placed in him and began a journey that led to my office that day. Along the way, he had learned to manage the emptiness and anger that boiled below the surface. But it was still there infecting every relationship he had ever known.

The façade of good manners and graciousness under fire had failed him many times, but not that day in my office. As Joel left I somehow knew that we were going to talk again. I'm not sure he had the same feeling.

Many years have come and gone since I met "that" Joel Engle. And I have had the privilege of watching the "real" Joel Engle emerge. We have walked together through some barren land and some times of bountiful harvest. We have challenged each other at the core of our beliefs like few friends I have ever known. The revelation of life that I have found through the process is worth every phone call, every email, and every friendly and challenging discussion along the way.

I am grateful that somehow, some way, the Lord allowed me to see Joel's heart that day we met. I pray that you too will have that privilege as you read this story of a godly man, well-acquainted with sorrow and rejection, who simply never gave up on becoming all God intends for him to be.

Stan Moser
President, Kingdom Men Ministries
www.kingdom-men.com/

1

PAIN AND DR. FRANK

Valerie was crying on the bathroom floor holding her arm. The fire of my rage was extinguished by a chill that slid through my body. My heart sank with the realization of what I had come to. This was my sweet, precious wife Valerie in pain on the floor—the first person to ever show me unconditional love.

I don't remember how the argument started. I do remember that I said something very cruel and she screamed in my face before running into the master bathroom and slamming the door. Then she locked it. After banging on the door for four or five minutes, I told her I was going to kick it in. She reluctantly opened it, and I burst through the door pointing my finger at her and yelling at the top of my lungs. She yelled back and turned away. I grabbed her arm and she pulled away, falling and hitting her arm on the sink.

"How did it get to this?" was all I could think as the tears and screams of emotional pain came out of my broken soul. How could I treat the most loving, sweet, beautiful, and intelligent person I have ever known with such selfishness and cruelty? What was wrong me with me? These questions had been racing through my mind through most of our meltdowns. The problem was that I didn't have any answers.

Don't think for a moment that I didn't love God. I loved God deeply. I loved Valerie deeply. I just had no idea how to control my temper. Rage is really a better word to describe it. I wanted to have the peace that I heard about in church—the peace that I heard Billy Graham talking about on TV. I was deeply ashamed. I didn't want to kill myself, but I did want to die. How could I be a Christian and feel that way? Valerie told me that I needed to seek counseling. I told her, "If reading the Bible and praying to God can't heal me, then nothing else will." I get sick when I think about that statement, but I really did believe that. What was wrong with me? Why couldn't I fix the horrible problem? Maybe Christianity doesn't work. I knew I was a true believer, even a minister of the gospel of Christ, but yet I couldn't seem to overcome those horrible feelings that led to my wife's tears on the bathroom floor.

I tried talking to several pastor friends of mine. One guy made fun of me. Another told me to just "cowboy up" and stop being a victim. A third guy just stared at me like a cow stares at a fence. That was the worst. It was hard to understand how a "man of God" had absolutely no clue what to tell me about the inconsistencies of my so-called Christian life. It only increased my sense of hopelessness. I was well-educated and bright, but very ignorant. So I went to see a "Christian counselor." One guy told me to pretend that my late mother was in a chair and talk to her. I cried like a baby, but three days later I was no different. Another told me that maybe I really wasn't a Christian. One lady told my wife to leave me. Someone else told me to memorize some Scriptures. I just kept spinning farther down the slope of shame.

It was quite obvious that things needed to change. There was no way that Valerie could live with my anger much longer. We had been married for a little over a year, and it is no exaggeration to say that marriage blindsided both of us. We expected problems but nothing of the magnitude of our "nuclear blow ups" that began to occur within the first weeks of our new life together. I was an unstoppable force of anger, she was an immovable object, and our daily collisions would result in mushroom clouds of bitterness and rage.

Our "fights" had been growing more intense by the week. Valerie was very independent and wanted to live her life her way, even if I wasn't involved. At times, I felt that she didn't even want to be around me. Of course, I wasn't that easy to be around. I was a control freak who tried to force my will down her throat.

On top of everything, I was traveling constantly as a Christian musician and had little space in my emotional life for the complexities of marriage. I was standing in front of thousands of people each week telling them about the hope of Jesus, even though my hope in Jesus was dissipating faster than the fizz of a Diet 7-up. I knew that my marriage was falling apart and that I was responsible for destroying one of the kindest people I had ever known. It was a lot like watching an episode of <u>Lost</u>: I had no idea what was going on or what was coming up next.

Something had to give. As I heard the weeping voice of my wife scream out in emotional pain, I hated myself and I knew that if something didn't change I was going to lose everything. I scheduled an appointment with a well-known Christian psychiatrist named Dr. Frank. Valerie came with me that first day so I wouldn't lie or skirt around any of the painful truth that needed to be dealt with in my life. I thought that I was a fraud. An impostor. I figured that Dr. Frank would have me thrown from the ministry forever and that I might even be excommunicated from Christianity.

I sat down in Dr. Frank's bland, stereotypical psychiatrist's office. There was the brown couch, the boring white walls with a plethora of degrees to show his credentials, and the large desk with two chairs on the "other side" of the table. My heart burned with anxiety, and my stomach was flipping with dread. I didn't want to be there, but where else could I go? I had run out of options.

Valerie sat next to me on the right. Finally the truth of my life was going to be exposed to someone other than Valerie, and I was terrified. I had made Valerie take a vow of secrecy to all her friends and family. No one could know. Now someone *would* know, and it was too late to turn back. As Dr. Frank listened, I began to unravel the sad story of my new marriage. I went on and on about what I had done—about the shame of my failure as a husband, Christian, and minister—about how I loved Valerie but would say incredibly hurtful things to her. Contrary to my dread-filled expectation of self-implosion, I actually began to feel much better. Yet when I would refer to the pain that I caused Valerie, my heart ached with regret. I closed my "confession" with this statement: "Dr. Frank, I am a fraud."

Dr. Frank didn't look like the sophisticated author and authority on Christian psychiatry that I expected. He wore cowboy boots and jeans with his white doctor's jacket. He was very friendly, and as he shook my hand I could feel the roughness of his calloused grip. When he spoke, his words twanged and drawled with a Texas accent. Overall, he lacked the pseudo-aristocratic polish I expected of one of the highly educated and famous pioneers of Christian psychiatry. He looked more like a farmer. He listened patiently, and when I was done he paused and looked at me. When he spoke, he said something to me that was so basic, yet so Spirit-filled that it still stirs my heart with emotion. "Joel," he said, "You are not a fraud. God loves you. Let me tell you something. Jesus Christ stepped out of history and into your life to make a difference."

To this day, I don't understand all of the ramifications of that statement, but it was revolutionary to me. God does love me, and it is Christ—the real, existing Christ—who makes the difference.

That was the beginning of my journey down a different road, a road that has led me to laughter, reverence, sorrow, joy, revelation, and peace. By no means have I figured out the mysteries of Christ or life, but I have found a Faithful Friend who really has made a difference. I don't know where you are right now, but I have a feeling you may have experienced a similar road to mine. You may be a person who loves God dearly but just can't seem to realize the Christian life in your daily experience. You may have objections to even the thought of the actual person of Jesus Christ. I don't know where you are exactly, but I'll bet you and I have some things in common. The emptiness and confusion that I endured for a great part of my life was real and painful. I don't mean to sound like I never had any good things happen to me. I have had many blessings—too many to mention. As a Christian, I had felt God's presence many times, and I had worked out a lot of my intellectual problems with God early on in my Christian life. Yet there were huge contradictions between my beliefs and my behavior. I also had some very misguided and incorrect convictions that kept me in the vicious cycle of frustration for many years. Yet I am here to tell you that God is real to me.

Here are a few things I want you to hang onto as we get to know each other.

1. God really does love you. You may not feel it, but it is true.
2. What you believe will determine how you behave.
3. You and I and the whole world have been destroyed by sin.
4. God has given every Christian all they will ever need to experience the abundant life in Jesus Christ.
5. You don't have to know everything to experience the power of God.
6. The Bible is God's source for truth and we must believe it in totality. I know that you might have a real problem with this one, but at least just try it on for awhile.

2

THE FIFTH WHEEL

I was born in San Francisco, California, where I went to a very prestigious private grade school. San Francisco is one of the most expensive places to live in America and most of the parents of my schoolmates were well off financially. My friends' houses had multiple rooms that were perfect for running around and having sleepovers, and sometimes it felt like visiting another world compared to the apartment I shared with my mother. You see, I didn't have a dad at home. I never met my dad; I never talked with my dad; I never even received a letter from my dad. From the bits and pieces of information I gathered over the years in my adult life, I learned that I was conceived out of wedlock. My mom rarely ever spoke of my biological dad when I was a kid. I think it was just too painful for her to talk about that relationship.

He was a lawyer, and my mom was a successful business woman. He was married, and my mom was not. Apparently my dad didn't want to deal with the scandal of having a child with a woman other than his wife, so he checked out of the relationship. Not long after that, my mom had a nervous breakdown. This is what I was told by people who knew the situation, anyway. So my mom gave birth to me and had to support a little boy in a very expensive city all by herself. Life's not fair, is it?

I will never forget going to my first "Father and Son" picnic that my grade school, Stuart Hall, sponsored. I hadn't given the whole thing a lot of thought until I drove up to the park with Anthony D'Amato and his dad. From the back seat of the car I could see all my schoolmates playing catch, running around, and having fun with their dads. I didn't want to get out of the car, but I did. I can still smell the grass of the park. The park had a bittersweet smell to it—a mixture of honey and coffee emanating from the grass and trees. I had a bittersweet feeling as well; I was glad to be with my friends, but I felt alone at the same time. I still feel that way whenever I think about it.

I guess I was an outsider from day one. I truly understand the whole "fifth wheel" concept. In fact, understanding the "fifth wheel" concept created my desire to feel significant. I was the super extrovert and class clown. I was ADHD before it was a word. Although I tested with a pretty decent IQ, I acted up at school and got in trouble for talking and fighting with other classmates. I just couldn't focus very long. It was like I was hardwired for TV. At school I couldn't sit still, but turn on *Gilligan's Island*, *The Brady Bunch*, or cartoons and I would be glued to my seat. And *Star Trek*—I just loved *Star Trek*. I daydreamed about what it would be like to have Captain Kirk as my dad. He could play catch with me and give me life lessons like how to handle Linda Lane, a cute fourth grader who tried to kiss me against my will. Captain Kirk knew how to handle the ladies. Or maybe he could teach me how to defend myself from the seventh grade bullies with one of his famous "judo chops." I lived in a fantasy world because my reality was scary. I felt so alone because I had so little control over my life. What if my mom died? Where would I go? Riding the municipal bus to school was a daily experience of having to be on alert from bigger boys who would pick on me. Getting made fun of at school for being "weird" was a weekly traumatizing experience. You see feeling like a chronic "fifth wheel" is a frightening feeling. I did whatever I could to be liked. The only problem was that it didn't work.

I remember when one of the kids in my class took a poll about me in art class. The poll was, "Do you like Joel Craddick?" Only one kid in my class voted for me, and that vote was probably because it was the Christian thing to do. The point is that I felt that nobody liked me, and this cruel "poll" was one of the incidents that crystallized it. That feeling of being on the outside has plagued me most of my life. It followed me to junior high, high school, and even college. I just couldn't break into the cool crowd.

The absence of my dad at home wasn't a big deal to me because I didn't know any different. I loved my mom. We had a tumultuous relationship, but I loved her, and she loved me the best that she could. Some might say, "How can you say not having a dad wasn't a big deal to you?" My reply is, "You don't miss what you don't have." I am not saying that I never wished for a dad to teach me things like riding a bike, how to box, and how to fish—you know, "man stuff." I was an "only child," so I wished for a dad in the sense that I wanted someone who could interact and play with me, who could take me on a boat ride in the Bay and teach me how to hit a baseball. However, functionally at least, my mom was really my dad anyway.

The idea of God as Father was not repugnant to me—at least not intellectually. My emotions were bothering me though. I didn't feel the love of God. Even though I believed in God at an early age, He was terrifying to me in some ways. Going to a Catholic school and experiencing the formalities and rituals of the Catholic Church was scary. The priest and his Latin were strange, the statue of Jesus hanging on the cross was pretty eerie, and the concept of Holy Communion—the fact that people were supposedly eating *flesh* and drinking *blood*—well, that was just plain weird. Since I wasn't an official Catholic, I was forbidden to participate in that ritual. One time I decided to get in on some of the action, and I ate a wafer. It was an unauthorized waver. Two nuns, my religion teacher, and my principal told me that I was probably going to go to hell for that. I have to admit that was slightly disarming for a kid of my age to hear. These pictures, events, and emotions created my concept of God. God was stern, distant and punitive, but I understood that and accepted it. You don't mess with God. I had no problem with that idea at all. I liked living, and wanted to do what I could to stay on His good side.

God never really gave me any reason to doubt His love, but I doubted anyways because many of my life experiences contradicted what the Bible or the church told me about God. Yes, there is definitely a good portion of Scripture that displays God's wrathful image, but there are plenty that describe His love as well. I just had a hard time feeling it. I felt His love at times, like when I went to Glorieta, New Mexico with my uncle to a missions conference. They had a youth camp going on at the same time called Centrifuge. That is the first time I remember hearing about God's love while also *feeling* it. The idea of God loving me was not something I thought about a whole lot until I went to the camp. There were two hundred kids there, and we would sing these incredible songs at the top of our lungs. In the midst of the worship and praise, I would feel what I thought to be God's love and reality. I spent many years trying to figure out why I couldn't feel the love of God in my "real life" like I did at that camp. I did so many bad things and had so many terrible thoughts that I really wondered how God could love someone so sinful and messed up. I think that I didn't want to really believe that God loved me because I was scared I would find out that He really didn't. I didn't want to get my hopes up.

Now, I don't like to be cliché, but it just happens that way sometimes. Everybody and their dog talks about God's grace and how we don't deserve it—how He gives it anyway. I just couldn't wrap my brain around that. It didn't register on the chart. I remember a particular bus ride in San Francisco from when I was a kid. I sat across from two Chinese ladies who were speaking in Mandarin to each other. I had no idea what they were saying, but at times I could sense the vibe of their conversation. That was God's love to me. I had no idea what it language it was in but every once and a while I got the vibe of it in my heart. All my life, in the very back of my mind, I wanted God to love me, but I just couldn't feel it or understand how He could love someone as "jacked-up" as me.

At this point I am sure that someone is saying, "Now Joel, you know that feelings fade, and then we have to believe God loves us by faith." I used to get mad at people in my youth group who would casually talk about God's love like talking about a TV show or something. You don't trivialize something that important.

You see, if God exists (and He does), then He must be holy and powerful. If he is holy and powerful and we are not (I know that for a fact), then our need for God's love—mercy included—is extraordinary. Without it we are condemned to hell and to lives devoid of hope or joy.

There's not even a need for me to lay down an argument for the sinfulness of man. Look at history. Watch CNN or Fox News. Replay every motive of your heart. We are messed up, and messed up bad. Whether it is the arrogant and ignorant business man on the golf course checking out the cart lady or the violent criminal in the back of a police car, we are all soiled by the stench of sin. We all desperately need God's love. My problem was I thought I was too wicked to ever get God's love. The whole idea of grace was like trigonometry to me. I just didn't get it—at least not for a long time.

One time, before I was a pastor, my pastor Ross Sawyers preaching through Romans, and as I listened to him teach through Chapter 5 a few years ago, a verse hit me really hard.

Romans 5:3-5 " . . . but we also rejoice in our afflictions, because we know that affliction produces endurance, endurance produces proven character, and proven character produces hope. This hope does not disappoint, because God's love has been poured out in our hearts through the Holy Spirit who was given to us."

There is more truth packed into this verse than rice and beans in a burrito from Chipotle. We can have joy in our afflictions? If that is the case, then I should be able to have a lot of joy! And I love hope. It is like drinking an ice cold Coke out of a glass bottle in the summer—utterly refreshing. Hope is a commodity that will never depreciate. It only becomes more valuable in life, especially as you grow older. Hope is like air; you suffocate without it.

The key line in that passage is that God's love has been "poured out into our hearts." God took the time to pour His love into my empty, dry, and despairing heart. You either believe this truth or you don't, and I have chosen to believe this. All of the moments of abandonment, pain, and loneliness I have experienced are redeemed for good in me because God "poured" His love into my life.

My whole life I wanted someone to chase me, to pursue me. I wanted to be picked at least third or fourth in kickball, but it never happened. Instead, I was almost always picked last. Sometimes I wasn't even picked at all; I just migrated over to a team hoping not to get turned away.

Nobody ever initiated any kind of relationship with me. I was damaged goods or something. Yet the God of the universe, the great King of kings, initiated a love relationship with me despite all of my pain, wickedness, and isolation. All of the hurt was for a reason. He was shaping me, molding me like clay. And I was useful clay, clay with purpose and meaning. I didn't even make first contact with God. He chose me. I don't have to be an isolated victim all alone and miserable. He picked me. It doesn't even matter in what order I was picked, because He "poured" His love into my heart. I know He loves me—I choose to believe it. I am too tired to try and deserve it anyways. It's good not to be the "fifth wheel" anymore.

3

ALL ALONE

M ost people from California don't go to Oklahoma for vacation. I don't think anybody goes to Oklahoma for vacation but me. The reason my mom and I would take vacations to Oklahoma is because that was where my grandparents lived. I loved going there. I would spend the whole summer with them before returning to California in August.

For some reason, my mother chose to live over 1,000 miles away from where she was raised. If you are from Oklahoma, you can't find a more opposite place to live than San Francisco. My mom and grandparents talked on the phone a quite a bit, but there was a distance in their relationship that exceeded the miles that separated them. My mom's only sibling, Jimmy, became a missionary and moved to Beirut, Lebanon. Okay, that is even more of an opposite place to live than Oklahoma. I think that my grandpa was very strict and my grandma was a control freak, which possibly resulted in the emotional coldness in my mom's relationship with them. So it was really weird when my mom wanted to come out to Oklahoma for a whole week to be with my grandparents and me, at the end of my annual, summer-long visit.

We had a great week together. My mom was laid back and happy, which was very different for her. She could be cruel sometimes. Often, the only thing she would say to me in the morning was, "Don't talk to me until I have a cigarette." That hurt me even though I laughed it off. That time in Oklahoma, she was fun, relaxed, and nice. We had a great time. It was an unusual time for us, and I didn't want it to end.

Standing on Grandma and Grandpa's porch, we said our goodbyes. I can still hear their front door squeak as Grandpa held it open. As we were preparing to leave, I remember Grandpa's voice beginning to tremble and his lower lip quivering.

"JoAnn, couldn't you stay a few more days?" Grandpa said to my mom.

"Dad, I have to go back to work. Maybe you can come out and see us soon?" Mom replied.

I really wanted to move to Oklahoma. I wanted to have a simpler, quieter life than the urban life of San Francisco. I wanted to smell the orchard on my grandparents' few acres. It was filled with peaches, apples, and blackberries. I would miss them. I would miss Tiger, the white cat, who always had scabs on his thin, pinkish ears. I would miss the McGee's pool. Most of all, I would miss Grandma and Grandpa. I still love them deeply, even though they've been gone a long time now.

Mom and I drove our rental car to Oklahoma City and flew home. As the plane prepared to land, I could see the fog outside the window of the plane. The Bay Bridge, Alcatraz, and the ocean were familiar sights that I took for granted.

There is nothing stranger than traveling from the heat of Oklahoma in August to the fog of San Francisco—going from 98 degrees to 51 degrees in a few hours. I remember feeling really lost as I returned home that afternoon—lost emotionally. I loved my grandparents and I hated leaving them. Wetumka, Oklahoma was a very safe place for me. My grandparents loved each other and they were crazy about me. Visiting people who are crazy about you makes you want to stop visiting and move in with them.

Driving from South San Francisco, I felt the hollowness of missing my grandparents. I cried a little bit, and my mom consoled me. It was cold and foggy. I still can't get over that. Cold and foggy in the summer—what a life! As we passed the Children's Hospital, we approached 29 Palm Avenue, our apartment building. It was a two-story blue building with a dumpy backyard and a two-car garage that we used with another tenant. We walked up the stairs and opened the door to our little home. Princess and Tiffy were waiting for us. Actually, they were waiting for my mom. Those cats hated me, but the feeling was mutual. This was home, but it was lonely without Grandma and Grandpa.

I went to bed that night after watching "Barney Miller" on TV. If you know the show "Barney Miller," then you are either old or you watch way too much *Nick-At-Nite*. My mom stood over my bed and said her familiar pre-bed anthem, "I love you more and more everyday." That night I could feel that kind of love. Yes, her love was imperfect, but I could feel it and I loved her, too. She was my mom.

The next morning I woke up at 7:27 a.m. I stared at my digital clock until I felt the pangs of early morning hunger dance in my stomach. I turned left outside of my room, walked down the narrow hallway, and turned right into the kitchen. I looked forward to the breakfast table, but then I saw something blue on the floor. I froze. I don't know why terror is cold, but it is. In an instant, the shock of ice-cold fear poured from the back of my head, down my chest, and into my heels. I was frozen in pure terror at what I saw.

My mom was on the floor. She looked like she might have been sleeping except she was breathing very hard. She had her blue bathrobe on, and I could see Princess walking around her, meowing for food. My mom's legs were jerking up and down. Not wildly but slightly. Everything was in slow motion as I leaned down on my knee beside my mom's face. Her face was covered with cat food because she had fallen into Princess' bowl. The word "Mom" choked out of my mouth like a missile from the bottom of my stomach. I screamed it the second time, but my mom wouldn't wake up.

I didn't know what to do. This was before 911 calls. I called the operator and in a panicked, manic way told them that my mom was unconscious. They were going to send an ambulance. I tried to call my grandparents in Wetumka, but nobody was answering. I went back into the kitchen to see if my mom had awakened. She was still asleep, so I ran to the front living room and opened up the bay window to yell for help. My neighbor, a young guy, was getting into his VW bug. I yelled at him, "Help me, my mom is unconscious!" He looked at me, shook his head, and got into his car and drove off. I screamed even louder. Finally, a lady from across the street heard me and asked me what was the matter. I told her, "My mom is unconscious, help me." She quickly ran across the street as the ambulance arrived. The neighbor lady with the blond hair, came up into my apartment just behind the paramedics. By that point I was hysterical, and she was trying to calm me down. After a few minutes, the paramedics told me that my mom had just passed out and she would be fine. In my heart, I knew differently.

There is something about our instincts that doesn't lie. Despite what the paramedics said, I knew that my mom's life was in jeopardy. The lady with blonde hair took me over to the hospital. I waited with her and another nurse in a cold, sterile waiting room. Cartoons were playing on the TV set, but I didn't care. All I could think about was my mom. Several hours later, I was asked to go into another room. They sent in the neurologist who was working on my mom. The second he walked into the room I knew my mom's fate. I could see it in his eyes. He told me that my mom had suffered a massive cerebral hemorrhage, a massive stroke. A blood vessel in her brain had exploded, and her brain was bleeding. He told me that they were doing everything they could to help her, but that was not a whole lot of consolation for me. I knew my mom was going to die. Don't ask me how, but I did.

As my meeting with the neurologist ended, I walked outside of the room. As I was walking outside, there was an elevator directly across from the door that I was walking past. The elevator was open and I saw two men pushing my mom's stretcher out from the elevator towards me. I remember the shock of seeing my mom, helpless, unconscious, and in a deep coma. I clutched the side railing of the stretcher she was laying on and cried, "Mom, I love you. Can you hear me? I love you." As the men wheeled my mom away, I asked the nurse if she thought my mom could hear me. She said yes. I don't know if my mom could hear me or not, but I hoped she could. I loved her. She was my mom.

I went back to the neighbor lady's apartment. On the way over, the song with the line *"if you want my body"* by Rod Stewart was playing on the radio. To this day, anytime I hear that song, I go right back to that terrible day. Isn't it weird how a song can do that? Or even a smell? When I got to her apartment, they gave me a sedative and tried to contact my grandparents. They finally found them. They had traveled about 50 miles from Wetumka to Ada,

Oklahoma to visit my Uncle Bill. When I woke up, they told me that my grandparents would be coming in that night. I just remember feeling so alone that day, stuck in a stranger's apartment. The apartment was dark and I felt lost among the unfamiliar people and furniture, wondering if I would ever see my mom again. I was begging God for my grandparents to arrive. I was literally shaking on a white couch, almost suffocating from the dread of finding out my mom might die. I could hear people talking to me, but nothing made sense. I wanted to run away, but at the same time I wanted them to stay. Things like that stick with you for the rest of your life. This was worse than feeling like a "fifth wheel." This was the feeling of death.

We are surrounded by death every day, and we don't even know it. Not just physical death, but the separation of our hearts from true life. Emptiness, loneliness, isolation— we are trapped in the shell of our consciousness. It's like being at a busy airport traveling alone. All of these people are around you, but you are alone. You don't talk to them, you don't know them, you are trapped inside your brain. We really are alone in this world. Just get over that fact. You can be married, single, dating or whatever, but you are alone. You are alive but separated from life. That is why we need God.

Talk about taking the initiative. God is alone but perfectly happy. He doesn't need anyone or anything. Yet He created us to have fellowship with Himself. He created a socket called our heart. If God is plugged into our sockets, we have a life-giving connection with Him. Our existence makes sense. If God is not connected to our heart, we are dead. Alive, but dead. We exist, but nothing makes sense, not death and not even life. If you take a good look at the world today, you can see that this is true.

1 John 1:3 "What we have seen and heard we also declare to you, so that you may have fellowship along with us; and indeed our fellowship is with the Father and with His Son Jesus Christ."

I know something about loneliness and isolation. We are not like God. We are not content to be alone. We don't like who we are no matter how often we try to tell ourselves that we are good. This is because we know that something is wrong. Instincts don't lie, but our brains do. God made us to have fellowship and a true connection with Him. Unless He plugs into the socket of our souls, we will never be alive. We can truly interact with God through Jesus Christ. I know this because I have experienced the life that God gives. He doesn't need me, but He chose me anyway. He who needs nothing has, by the sovereign act of His will, chosen to love me. This is Christianity. This is life.

4

AFRAID

D ogs freak me out for some reason. My good friends
Stan and Sue have a dog named Annie who is very
sweet for a dog—affectionate to a fault. She jumps up and
down all the time and skids across their wooden floors with
reckless ease. However, she still slobbers and smells like
a dog. I don't roll with dog slobber. Some of my friends
say that I am afraid of dogs, but I am a tough guy and will
never admit that as a fact. Actually, I am afraid of a lot of
things because I know that we live in a dangerous world.
We want to control our small parameters of existence by
self-protection because death surrounds us. I don't think
I am going to be killed by a little fluffy dog, but I do think
that the residual effects of the fear of death taint much of
our lives.

Fear is a powerful force in nature. We live in constant
fear: fear of failing in our careers, achievements, or
relationships; fear of dying; fear of war; fear of collapse;
fear of being poor—it is all around us. Why do you think
over half of all TV shows center on death and crime? We
are trying to water down our fears. Some people drive
Hummers because they are afraid that people won't think
they are rich, even if in reality they are one step away from
bankruptcy. I played golf with a guy who was sorely afraid

of being killed by an errant golf ball. I think he was in the wrong sport. I think my lousy golf swing expanded his fears greatly. Teenagers are afraid of being made fun of at school. We are marinated in fear.

We never know when our fears will be realized. All we know is that the day is coming. When my mom would come home two hours later than she said she would, I always wondered if something happened to her. Even though I was a kid, I could do the math. Two minus one equals one. If Mom died, I would be all alone in the world. I wasn't stupid, I knew the possibilities. However, I never thought the possibilities would become stark realities. I was dead wrong.

Two nights after my mom collapsed, I remember waking up afraid. The second I woke up I began to sob, crying out of fear of losing my mom. The vast weight of sorrow, mixed with fear and a sliver of hope, pressed hard upon my 11-year-old heart.

My grandparents had arrived from Oklahoma late the night before. They wouldn't let me see my mom, but I was in no condition to see her anyway. I wonder what my grandparents must have been thinking. To be in your late seventies and to see your little daughter in a coma has to be surreal. We waited and waited for the phone to ring and offer even a glimmer of hope.

I will never forget my religion teacher from school coming over to the apartment to comfort me. Miss Doris was an extremely nice lady who always had a smile and was very kind to me. My grandparents didn't know how to address my anxiety and fear, so they thought Miss Doris could help me. I asked her, "Do you think I will see my mom in heaven if she dies?"

Miss Doris replied, "Joel, there is no heaven. This is all there is."

Even though I was just eleven, that statement coming out of Miss Doris's mouth shocked me. I didn't expect such a cynical statement coming from my sweet religion teacher at Stuart Hall. I didn't believe her, though. My instincts told me that heaven and hell existed. I had no real theological predisposition at that time, but I just knew there was more than life on Earth.

We received the call on Sunday morning. I woke up and rode over to the hospital with my grandparents. I felt the weight of dread pushing in my chest like a 250 lb man sitting on my tiny little frame. My legs were literally shaking from intense apprehension and disbelief. "How could this be happening to me. What did I do to God to bring this on myself? Why me?" were the many questions flying through my eleven-year-old mind at light speed. We walked into the ICU with my mom's best friend, Terry Grant. There was a waiting room across the hall from where my mom was. I could see my mom through the glass window of the intensive care unit. She didn't look alive. She was in a light blue hospital gown with huge machines next to her, several tubes coming out of her mouth and arms. It was very hard to see. My mom was such a vibrant, funny, and loud person. It was surreal to see her chest move up and down as the ventilator filled her lungs with air. Her eyes were closed, and as I watched all those machines trying to keep her alive I felt hopeless, helpless, and extremely depressed.

As I walked into the waiting room across from where my mom was, I was introduced to different doctor than the one I met four days before. He was younger and taller, but had the same distressed look on his face. His expression made my heart start pounding. My head felt like someone was playing the drums inside of it. He told me that he was sorry for the news he was about to give me.

"Joel, your mom has thirty minutes to live," said the doctor.

I turned around to face my grandparents and Terry. "Your mom is a fighter, Joel," said Terry. "If she could fight any more, she would." I knew it was true, but it didn't make me feel any better.

I remember watching with dismay when the first video clips of the Tsunami in Sri Lanka were put on air, which was just after Christmas in 2004. I was in Peoria, Illinois doing music for a large youth conference. As I watched the videos, I was faced with the sheer power of destruction that a huge body of water could cause. It was staggering. When they told me that my mom only had thirty minutes to live, a tsunami of sorrow rushed over me. My legs gave out, and I was overcome with tears and pain. They had to carry me to the car.

Thirty minutes later my mom died.

The first words that choked out of my mouth were, "God, I hate you!" I really didn't know what else to say. I knew that God existed, and I knew that He could have saved my mom if He had wanted to, but He didn't.

Somehow, sometime, we will see some of our deepest fears become life experiences. It is just the way the universe works. Blame it on sin. Blame it on God. Blame it on Satan. The blame doesn't change the reality. We live in a dark world filled with fear—not just paranoia, but *real* fear. Bad things happen to people, and we are afraid that they may happen to us. Jesus Christ was a real person who lived in a real world filled with death, pain, and harsh realities. The Bible calls Jesus a "**Dawn from on high**" who will "**shine on those who live in darkness and the shadow of death.**" It also says that Jesus will "**guide our feet into the way of peace.**" (Luke 1:78-79) Jesus himself claimed to be the "light of the world." In our dark world it is impossible to see hope apart from the love of Jesus Christ. Light is a natural agent that helps us see. Without it we are in the dark and locked in the blackness of our fears—not able to see our reason for existence or any hope at all. When we can't see hope, we become filled with anxiety. Peace is the opposite of fear, and Christ leads us to peace. It is His love that draws us onto the way of peace.

You may ask, "If God is so loving, then why did He let your mom die?" I don't know the answer to that. All I can tell you is that from where I stand now, the love of Jesus Christ has led me to peace and has made my life meaningful, even in the midst of intense emotional pain. Jesus is more real to me than drinking Diet Coke. I am not saying that I don't struggle with pain, because that would be a lie. I struggle with pain and fear, but I am not hopeless anymore. The "Dawn" has broken into my life, and He has led me to peace. The more I know Him, the more I love Him and the more I know that He loves me. I don't deserve His love, but He gives it to me anyway.

I still miss my mom. It has been 27 years since she died, but sometimes it feels like yesterday. I have lived in the "shadow of death" in my lifetime. Sometimes that shadow felt more like a black hole. Yet, even now I can feel the love of God shining down on me. I know He loves me. I know He loves you. I have chosen to believe this as an immutable truth. I don't always feel it, but I do feel it now. I used to run from trying to feel God's love because I didn't want to get let down. That was fear controlling my life. Now I am happy to take whatever feelings He allows me to have. Even a runner like me gets tired of running.

5

CHICKEN FAJITAS AND GOD

L et me try to explain to you the magnificence of Uncle Julio's chicken fajitas. Uncle Julio's is a small chain of Mexican restaurants in the Dallas/Fort Worth metroplex. If you have never been to Uncle Julio's, then you have never really had chicken fajitas—you have been eating something impersonating a chicken fajita. The only reason I can give for my opinion is that I have tasted the fajitas from Uncle Julio's, and there has never been one chicken fajita elsewhere that compares. You should just go there and find out for yourself. Tell them Joel sent you.

Trying to explain to you what God has done in my life is nearly impossible because you were not there to see it. I mean, I still have some seriously bad issues that I deal with on a daily basis, but there has been a significant change in my happiness and contentment because I know Jesus Christ. By the way, that doesn't mean that there are no moral absolutes, because I deeply believe there are. There are some people that will try to sell you the illogical concept that morality is based on your view of life and that no one should "impose" their view of right and wrong on other people. I believe the truths of the Bible are immutable and unchanging. I want to take you into my life experiences so you can see what Christ has done in me, then maybe you can understand what He wants to do in your life.

If you have never been to San Francisco, then you have missed something great. The city is like no other city on earth. I can still smell the eucalyptus trees. They smell like a mixture of lemon and honey. If I try hard enough I can hear the ocean breaking on Bakers Beach. I can feel the misty salt air sprinkle my face as I walk along the pier. From the immaculate beauty of the Golden Gate Bridge to the abundance of great restaurants, San Francisco has the corner on cool and on natural elegance.

Yet there is something about Wetumka, Oklahoma that is alluring as well. It is definitely not the ocean. It does have some trees, though it smells more like hay than lemon and honey. I can hear the million-voiced choir of locusts preparing for nightfall in the summer. I can see the red dirt on Sleepy Valley Lane. I can go onto Main Street and see Otho Little's meat market. It is gone now, but I can still picture it.

Moving from San Francisco to Wetumka is like jumping into an ice-cold swimming pool in the wintertime. It is quite a shock to your system. You don't hear twenty-five different languages on the bus in Wetumka, but you also don't hear anybody speak Creek Indian in San Francisco. The accents are different. The speed is different. The people are different as well.

I remember going to see my mom's body at the funeral home in Wetumka. I climbed out of the black limousine and slowly walked up the stairs. As I looked through the window of the front door, I could see my mom's face. She was in her casket. I stopped for a moment because of the overwhelming reality of my mom's death. She really was gone. My grandma and grandpa sobbed with anguish. I was too scared to cry.

As I walked into the room where my mother's body was, I approached her face. It is impossible to explain with words what it is like to know that you will never see your mother's face again. That was the last time. The funeral home people put a smile on my mom's face. There was a really weird smell in the air—a serious smell, a perfume that contained a somber yet spicy fragrance. I hope I never smell that again. There was my mom, one of the funniest and most physically attractive people I have ever known. She was smart and sarcastic. I remember her laugh, high-pitched and song-like. It was like someone practicing singing scales but laughing them instead of singing them. I loved that laugh. As I looked down, I knew she wasn't really there. Her soul was gone.

We had a funeral, and that was it. My mom was gone, and the world kept on moving. I really thought that the world should just stop and show some respect, but it didn't. It never does. That is just the way it is. Life is but a quick sneeze, and then it is over.

I had to keep on living, and I was to live in Oklahoma. My grandparents made me go to church and school. Neither of them were very different from the other. They were both boring and highly structured. At least at church I could sleep during the sermon. My grandparents were Southern Baptists and went to First Baptist Church, Wetumka. It was a simple and solid church, I just didn't like going. It was scary in a different kind of way. The preacher preached as if he was really upset. He would wave his hands all around and yell with a seemlying angry voice. I was definitely not used to that in church coming from a semi-Catholic background. That changed later on, but when I first got there I really thought he was mad at us.

My interpretation of church was kind of like Charlie Brown at school. Every time you see Charlie Brown when he is in school, the teacher's voice is muffled and it sounds like they are talking underwater. That was church to me, just a bunch of noise that I didn't understand and most certainly did not enjoy.

What I enjoyed about First Baptist Wetumka was the sense of community. I really did feel like I belonged there. There was no power point or video screen projecting song lyrics or verses. There was no band, just an organist and a piano. We sang hymns—good hymns. The preaching was pretty good, but I don't remember one sermon. Not to demean preaching. Preaching is important, huge even, but I don't remember one single sermon from First Baptist Wetumka. I remember the smile of Louise MacFarland though. She was super, over-the-top nice. She would always go out of her way to talk to me and she would gently hug me and tell me what a "nice-looking" young man I was. I remember Teresa and Dawn from the youth group. They were great. Teresa came over to my house when my grandpa died. What comforted me is that Teresa cared enough to take the time to see how I was doing. She made me feel like I mattered. And she was very cute too! I still remember that. Even though our preacher, Reed Lynn, loved Southern Gospel music and was ultra conservative, he really did take the time to befriend me.

I distinctly remember Bill Wilkerson. He came over to my house to take me to church on Wednesday nights and occasionally on Sunday. Mr. Wilkerson was a pig farmer and water commissioner for the county, and he was incredibly kind. He was not a theologian or some fancy religious dignitary, but he was one of the greatest Christians I have ever met. To me that is what church is really about—real relationships with real people.

So I loved the people, but I had a hard time connecting with the boring sermons of the church. Then Terry

Goodwin asked me if I wanted to go to church camp. I was 12 years old and it was around 1980. He was a pretty cool kid, but I really had reservations about going. What finally convinced me was the fact that girls would be there. And I actually found one that liked me! We walked around the really large campground every day, hardly saying five words to each other, but we "liked" each other. Then she dumped me at the end of the week for a guy in her youth group. You can't compete against a guy who is on the inside.

Church camp was a lot of fun, but I almost got sent home on the very first day. Our preacher told us that we were forbidden to go into the dorm rooms of the opposite sex. Before bedtime on the first night, I was running up the stairs when the girls grabbed my arm and pulled me into their dorm. I am not exaggerating or being sarcastic—they pulled me in. Out of nowhere, I heard my preacher's voice say, "Joel Craddick you have broken the rules that have been established. You are expelled from the premises of Falls Creek Baptist Assembly." This was no Charlie Brown in the classroom moment. I heard that loud and clear. I was scared out of my mind!

I can cover myself pretty good. Okay, more than just pretty good. I am a professional at covering myself. I don't know what I said that day to my preacher, but it worked and I convinced him to let me stay. I am glad that I did. It was a great place—not the boring place I thought it was going to be. Falls Creek is still in my heart and I have had the privilege of going back and leading worship music for the 5000 campers there several times. Nobody ever pulled me into the girl's dorm again either.

Later that week at camp, sitting somewhere in the center of the huge outdoor pavilion called "the tabernacle," I was sweating. Falls Creek is hot and humid. Back in the day, everybody carved something into the back of the wooden pews at Falls Creek, and I was probably carving when Terry Goodwin told me I needed to "get saved." You have to understand that I had no idea what that meant. For Terry, that meant that when the camp preacher stopped yelling and the music began, you followed the girls to the front of the auditorium. I had no problem at all with that! They sang a hymn called "Wherever He Leads I'll Go," and it was intoxicating. There was real emotion, and I could feel it. To this day I believe it was the first time I ever felt the presence of the Holy Spirit. I am not saying that I knew it was the Holy Spirit, but what I felt was more than just group dynamics. It was as if the Holy Spirit was speaking to only me in the midst of five thousand people. Somehow and some way God was using my emotions to communicate that I mattered to Him. I just didn't understand the gospel at that point. What I really wanted was to belong somewhere.

When they took all of the people who had come down to the front of the tabernacle over to the counseling rooms, I was in the herd of preteens. Some large pastor with a huge belt buckle the size of Arkansas greeted me and led me to two metal chairs inside the counseling area. The only thing that I remember about our conversation was the question, "Do you want to go to heaven or hell?" My answer was obvious. That question is like asking someone, "Do you want to be filthy rich or get beaten with a baseball bat?" So I mechanically prayed the "prayer" and asked God to "save" me. I had no idea what I was doing but I really didn't want to screw this opportunity up. After that night I was "officially" a part of the system. I belonged to the club. I was "in." At the same time, there was a huge disconnect in my heart. I was a pretty smart kid and I felt like this whole thing was way too easy and unclear. I felt pressure to "do the right thing" rather than to really think my decision through. I felt like they were too quick to sign me up, dunk me, and process me through. It's like what you do with pancakes. When you cook them, you want to serve them immediately before they get cold and lousy. I felt like I was treated like a hot pancake. "We had better sign him up before he cools off." There was something artificial and uninspiring about the whole thing. I was now religious. But I really wasn't. What I really wanted was my mom and a place to belong.

I had experienced religion but not the real, historical Jesus Christ. Like eating chicken fajitas at Chilli's, I thought I had tasted the real thing. That is, until I ate at Uncle Julio's.

Psalm 34:8 "Taste and see that the Lord is good; blessed is the man who takes refuge in him."

6

THE GOD THAT SLEEPS IN YOUR ROOM

I really didn't know what racism was until I moved to Oklahoma. That is not to say that there wasn't racism in San Francisco. There was, and it was just as bad as it was in Oklahoma; I just didn't know it until I got older. Wetumka is broken down into three races: black people, Indian people, and white people. The white people had the money and lived on the east side of the railroad tracks, everybody else lived on the west side. Believe it or not, the kids in Wetumka were way tougher than the kids in San Francisco. The only fight I ever got into in San Francisco was with Craig Fenton. He kicked me in the shins so I pushed him. I really thought that was a pretty violent fight, but my view of fighting was about to radically change.

I just didn't fit in at all in Wetumka. In fact, I stuck out like a salad at a chicken fried steak convention. I got in my very first fistfight with Danny Heathcott a few weeks after I moved to Oklahoma. The UFC would easily have wanted the rights to broadcast that fight. Fists flew between us from one end of our classroom to the other. In eighth grade, I got into another fight with a kid named Jeff Yahola, and I found out what it meant to see "stars" after getting punched in the face. Honestly, I have no idea how many fights I actually got into because I have lost count over the years—probably somewhere around eleven or twelve. Violence is wrong and I never want to condone the violent past of my life. Yet, somehow my experiences of having to survive my mom's death and the reality of being an orphan formed the attitude of a warrior in me. This attitude wasn't motivated by courage, but by fear. I was determined to make it in life, and I was willing to work hard and do what I had to do to survive. However, on the inside of my heart I was very, very afraid.

When I became a Christian (probably in eighth grade), I had no idea how to relate to God. By that time, the only male relationship that I had was with my grandfather. My grandpa was a great man. He was the superintendent of schools and probably the most respected man in Hughes County. Grandpa was a dignified man who treated people with kindness and respect. He didn't talk much, but he had a grandpa's sense of humor. He played with me and made train noises on command. We would be driving down the road in Scout, my grandpa's truck, and he would make the train noises. I loved that. My grandpa took me to the McGee's swimming pool across the highway in 100-degree heat. He was a very good grandpa.

I was 11 years old when I came to live with Grandma and Grandpa. Something changed in our relationship—it was no longer like it was during the summer visits. Before, I was their special, California grandson. Now I was the orphaned, troubled preteen, and they had no idea how to handle me. Once again I felt like a "fifth wheel."

Grandma, by instinct, hovered over me like a mother hen and constantly brought up the desires that my mom had for my well-being. "Your mother made me promise to brush your teeth every day," she would say. "I promised your mother that you would never ride your bike on the road." This drove me crazy, and I began to have bitter feelings towards my grandma. I should have been more understanding, but I was a child, and to most children understanding others is a foreign concept.

I would respond to my grandma's overprotective nature with anger. In later years, my grandpa would react. It got to the point where he punched me once, but by then I was old enough to fight back. I remember hitting my grandpa and watching him fall to the ground. This memory has haunted my life ever since that day. I hurt the one man I really loved and respected. What kind of person would hit their grandpa? How could God ever love me?

Maybe part of the problem was that I wanted my mom to mother me, not my grandma.

I remember lying in bed the day after my mom died. My grandma was sitting on the side of my bed, and I couldn't stop crying.

"I want my mom," I said over and over again. My mind was set on a loop of wanting my mom there beside me.

My grandma gently touched my back and said, "Wishing for your mom is like wishing for the moon. You just can't have it."

Don't judge her too quickly for that statement. She had just lost her daughter. She had also survived the flu pandemic of 1918, both World Wars, the Great Depression, and the Cold War. Her generation had to deal with death and stress way more than we did.

When I first moved in with my grandparents, I slept in the front guest room. One night a few weeks after my mom's death, I had a nightmare where I dreamt that she came back from the dead. There was a bathroom between the front bedroom and my grandparents' room in the middle of the house. In the dream, my mom was in the bathroom with her back to me. Then she turned around with the most evil look in her eyes. When I woke up, I was terrified and sobbing. From that day on, my grandpa or grandma slept with me in my bed until they built my room on the other side of the house. I couldn't sleep alone. Sometimes I couldn't bathe by myself and would have to have my grandpa work security outside of the door of the bathroom. I was enslaved to fear.

When my new room was built, it quickly became my haven. From the day that I first moved in, it was my little world—a place where I felt in control. I began to isolate myself thereafter. My grandparents watched television from about 6 to 10:15 p.m. every night. When the weather report was over, they would go to bed. I spent most of that time in my room. There wasn't a whole lot of talking going on, but they did talk in bed for about 20 minutes every night. Sometimes I would listen to them from my room. They really did love each other, and I loved them; I was just afraid to come out of my room.

Brian Wilson from the Beach Boys wrote a song about his room. It was the place where he felt he could be real and free. I can relate to that, because my room was just about the only place that I could feel peace. I would listen to music, pretend to kiss girls (using my pillow), and draw pictures of things and people. I had created my own little world that I could control. I could do what I wanted to and didn't have to deal with people. In my room, I was the cool kid at school—the superhero—I could listen to the radio and sing along without feeling like a sissy. There were no conflicts with grandma or grandpa when I was alone in my room.

When I was 12 years old, I became obsessed with pro wrestling. I bought the magazines and watched it on TV religiously. For a season, I really wanted to be a pro wrestler. I had many successful bouts in my room. I defeated some of the toughest imaginary wrestlers in the history of the sport in my room. When I was in my room, nobody could push me around. The problem was that I couldn't stay there all the time. I had to leave my room for meals and school.

My room also was where I began to spend time with God. I would read endless amounts of the Bible in my room. I would talk to God "as one talks with a friend" in my room. It just seemed like my life fell apart when I had to leave my room. When I left to go to school, I would get made fun of and have to stand up for my "respect-factor" with the guys. When I left my room and interacted with my grandma, she would try to control me, which would make me explode with deep-seeded anger and cursing. Then my grandpa would respond with a serious spanking or even a beat-down. Sometimes I ran out of the house and actually climbed on top of the roof or the huge pecan tree in our backyard. Sometimes I would fight back. It still breaks my heart that it came down to that because I loved my grandpa more than anyone (except the Lord) could ever know. I felt that I was a terrible person and it was just best for everybody else if I stayed in my room. It seemed that the only time I acted like a Christian was in my room because I couldn't translate my relationship with God in the real world. I had no idea how to do that even though I really wanted to. My room was where I felt I could manage my fear and anger.

At night, however, my room changed. The fears would come, and I would be terrified that my mom would come back to haunt me. I know that sounds weird, but it is true. My grandpa would sleep in the twin bed across from my bed. We had a boxed air conditioner over his bed in my room that was on all night long. When Grandpa or sometimes Grandma was with me at night and that air-conditioner was humming, I wasn't afraid.

Fear is a tyrant. You know, they say that horses and dogs can sense when you are afraid. Fear senses when you are afraid too. It can spread very quickly in your life. I was enslaved to fear at night. I am not anymore, though. I think it changed when I began to realize that God was real and that He was sovereign. King David experienced fear, too. I love this verse that he wrote: **"When I am afraid, I will trust in You. In God, whose word I praise, in God I trust; I will not fear. What can man do to me?" (Psalm 56:3-4)**

Before I really believed in God, I was a water boy to fear. When I was afraid, I would panic and do whatever fear told me to do. Now that I know there is a God and that God is all-powerful and ever-present, I have nothing to fear. I trust in His protection. I don't even fear death as much. Why? Because God promised me that if I trusted in Jesus and His death on the cross to cover my sins, my future was heaven, not hell. It is not guesswork anymore. He either keeps His word or He is not God. That doesn't mean that I won't die a horrible death. It just means that even if I do, God is going to be there waiting for me.

God sleeps in my room with me now. Okay, I sleep and He is awake. But He is there now. I know it. Paul experienced more opportunities for fear than most of us. I find it interesting how he responded to it.

Romans 8:31-35 "What, then, shall we say in response to this? If God is for us, who can be against us? He who did not spare His own Son, but gave Him up for us all—how will He not also, along with Him, graciously give us all things? Who will bring any charge against those whom God has chosen? It is God who justifies. Who is he that condemns? Christ Jesus, who

died—more than that, who was raised to life—is at the right hand of God and is also interceding for us.

Who shall separate us from the love of Christ? Shall trouble or hardship or persecution or famine or nakedness or danger or sword?"

Like I said before, we either believe this or not. God is for me. He gave up His own Son to rescue me from my hopelessness, and He has given me more than I can even try to tell you. Jesus has put up holy fists for me against the bullies of fear and death. Nothing can separate me from Him. Nothing.

7

THE GOSPEL OF A HOPELESS CHRISTMAS

I am going to hit "pause" for a second and address something. There may be some intellectuals reading this and wondering where are all of my arguments for the validity of Christianity. I have learned them fairly well; I just don't think they have *that* huge of an impact. Romans 1:16 says that *the gospel* is the power of salvation—not rational arguments for the existence of God. I do believe that Christianity is rational up to a certain point, but it is the gospel (i.e. the cross and resurrection) that contains the power.

I love and respect theology. I would like to think of myself as a theologian, but then I read Jonathan Edwards, John Piper, and A.W. Tozer and realize that I am basically an idiot. If you want hardcore theology, start with those guys. Although I love reading them, I don't even feel worthy to quote them, much less try to emulate them. But if you want to see how the power of the gospel has changed my life, then keep reading.

There may be some who read this and think I am a religious fool. I am. But I would rather be a religious fool in heaven than a smart atheist in hell. I don't intend to sound unloving, but I really mean that. Sometimes we have to be fools in order to be wise.

1 Corinthians 1:27 "Instead, God has chosen the world's foolish things to shame the wise"

I just want to be real and believe in something real. I don't care if that makes me a fool in the world's eyes.

The first Christmas after my mom died was the hardest. For a kid, Christmastime is everything. It is the apex of all that is good and just in the world. Christmas trees, snow (except for warm climates), bad homemade candy, and carols are just gravy compared to the exhilaration of opening up fresh presents on Christmas morning. It is the only time of the year that a child would willingly get up at 5:00 a.m. Greed is a powerful thing, especially if it involves wrapping paper.

At least it *should* be the biggest day of the year for a kid. I tried to get excited about Christmas, but I couldn't. I remember watching some stupid show where the guy that played Gomer Pyle sang the song "All I Want for Christmas Is My Two Front Teeth." All I wanted was my mom. I still do in some ways. Instead, all I had in this world were my grandma and grandpa.

I miss my grandma's cooking. She would make me pancakes in the shape of cows, chickens, Grandpa or anything else. I miss the smell of Aqua-Net—her hairspray. I miss listening to her sing and do crossword puzzles. I wish I could go back in time and do some things over. I would have treated her much better, and I would have told her I loved her more than I did.

I miss my grandpa's cowboy hat and the spider-web wrinkles on his neck. I miss watching him fall asleep in his green lounge chair. I miss the way he smelled after he worked in the garden. It was like a combination of Old Spice, sweat, and sugary red Oklahoma dirt. I miss the train noises he would make. I miss watching him fall asleep in his green lounge chair. He was a big man and a real man.

Today, I did a radio interview and the host of the show asked me what kind of spiritual heritage my grandparents passed down to me. I don't remember a formal spiritual lesson they gave me, but I do remember learning from their lives. My grandpa read his Bible, and my grandma did, too. They didn't talk about original sin, predestination, or the substitutionary death of Christ, but it didn't matter because truth is caught more than it is taught. I know from their lives that they loved and feared God in the right way.

There are two distinct spiritual moments that I remember from my life with my grandfather. Grandpa didn't talk much. He preferred a brief "uh-huh" over some drawn out response. He let my grandma do most of the talking, and she was quite good at it. Maybe that is why these two instances left such a vivid impression on me.

The first one was at the end of a week-long revival at our church led by Anson Justice. You have never heard "fire and brimstone" preaching like Anson Justice preached. He was in his 80's when I heard him, and he preached the Bible with passion. I was the only kid in the youth group that liked it. I hesitate to say that I liked the fire and brimstone preaching because most of the people my age and younger hate it. I guess it's just that I hate pretense. I hate self-righteous pretense, and I hate grace-abusing pretense.

That week was the only time I can remember our church really having revival. People's lives were being changed. I saw 65-year-old men and women repent for their spiritual apathy and hypocrisy. I saw my 81-year-old grandpa go down to the front, broken over his casual Christianity. He didn't miss church after that. He was changed. He never talked to me about it, but I knew God did something in his life. My grandpa knew that I knew as well.

The second spiritual moment I remember is when my grandfather and I went to the Chieftain drive-in for a hamburger. It's funny; my grandpa would always put on a suit and a fedora hat to go one mile into town. Times have definitely changed.

We were driving out of the Chieftain parking lot, and I asked Grandpa the question, "Grandpa, if you died, do you know if you will go to heaven?"

Grandpa replied, "Joel, I do know that I will go to heaven because I put my faith in Jesus Christ."

I am so glad I asked that question. Two days later my grandpa died.

You may say to me, "I respect that your grandpa had faith in Jesus, but what makes that right and all other religions wrong?" I guess the only thing I can tell you is that out of all the religions I have studied, none of them seem to deal with the problem of sin in any honest manner. Christianity, real Bible-based Christianity, is about as real as you can get. Here is a quick synopsis of what the Bible says. For a more detailed understanding, please read Romans 1-5. Paul explains this way better than I do.

1. Man is sinful.
2. God is just and will punish sin.
3. Somehow God loves man and desired to save people from every nation, tribe, and tongue.
4. God sent Jesus (His Son) to take our punishment upon Himself, based solely on His love and merciful disposition towards us.

We all know that man is sinful, that man is not intrinsically good. It's just plain intellectually dishonest to believe otherwise. Mankind's motives are self-seeking and self-serving, especially compared to God's. God is holy—morally perfect in every way. He always makes the right decision, infinitely more than all of man put together—even when you include Jack Bauer. His motives are always pure. God must punish sin because he is the final judge and He always does the right thing. Yet, He created a way, even before the beginning of time, to rescue His people from certain destruction. He sent His most perfect Son, Jesus Christ, to live the perfect life and take our death penalty upon Himself. This way God's justice is proved right, and His love is displayed to all generations. What separates all other religions from Christianity is the work of Jesus. That is why Islam, Mormonism, the *Da Vinci Code*, and other religions try to distort the nature of Christ and the significance of the cross.

To me, the essence of the gospel (meaning good news) is found in Romans 5:8:

But God proves His own love for us in that while we were still sinners, Christ died for us!

I have experienced many hopeless Christmas' in my life. Watching everybody laugh and sing songs and open presents while I mimicked enjoying the season; but I was just acting. I felt lonely and missed my mom. Then I missed my grandpa. Then I missed my grandma. Yet, what gives me legitimate hope is the possibility that God really does love me. He doesn't love me because I am an awesome miracle of a human-being. He doesn't love me because He has a soft spot in His heart for total screw up's like me. God loves me because Jesus reconciled my sin and rebellion towards God and the world by taking my place on the cross. God proved His love for me by sending the greatest gift that supersedes any Christmas present the world could offer. He sent Jesus because He loved and chose to redeem His fallen children who had no possibility of escaping the destruction of their sin.

You've gotta love that Scripture! What hope! Hope even for a messed-up kid like I was. Hope for you, too. Even in the middle of a hopeless Christmas and amid the aching loss of my grandparents, I still could have hope. I follow in the faith of my grandpa and my grandma, but my faith is still my own. Maybe I am a fool, but if being a fool means loving Jesus, then I don't want to be wise.

This true story is how the gospel has worked in my life. I am far, far from perfect in applying these truths to my daily life. But you know what? I don't have anymore hopeless Christmases because I have a hope that will never leave. If you don't have this hope, I sincerely pray that God will open your eyes, ears, and heart to see Jesus for who He really is.

8

HOSPITALS

I don't like hospitals. They are so white and dull, so serious and crabby. At least most hospital people are crabby—it's probably the bedpans. I would be crabby, too, if I had to change out your bedpan. Hospitals are cold. They give you one sheet to cover yourself with, and you always have to ask for more. The food is terrible. They think they can make up for the bad food by including red Jell-O. It almost works.

When you go to the hospital, you are supposed to rest. That's why you are in bed all the time. However, you can't rest because they come in every three hours to take your vitals, give you a shot, or administer some medicine. Like I said, I don't like hospitals.

I have been in the hospital four times. The first for pneumonia. The second time for what they call an orchidopexy. I remember my mom crying as they took me into the operating room. I told her that I would be fine, which was pretty brave—especially knowing what an orchidopexy actually entailed. It is about the most painful operation a member of the male gender can have. One of the nurses called me "a little soldier." I think she had a crush on me to be quite honest with you, even though I was seven.

The third time I was in the hospital was for an emergency appendectomy. They said that my appendix exploded the second they took it out of me. Cool. I was in the hospital for about five days, and I received a lot of sympathy from the girls at school. It was worth the whole thing if you ask me.

The last time I was in the hospital was due to food poisoning. I had the double-cooked pork at The House of Wang. I should have known better. I threw up seventeen times and almost died. They put a tube up my nose and down my throat into my stomach. Now you know why I hate hospitals.

But as bad as it is to be hospitalized, nothing quite matches the pain and difficulty of visiting loved ones in the hospital.

It was a Saturday morning in Wetumka. The October air was chilly but energizing. The leaves had been brown for awhile, and they littered the ground all around our acreage. I heard a knock on my bedroom door from my grandma. She opened the door and very casually said, "Grandpa is sick. We need to go to the doctor."

She told me that Jack McGee, our neighbor, had taken Grandpa to the hospital. "That's weird," I thought to myself. I wondered why Grandpa couldn't take himself. I remembered that all that week Grandpa had been pretty lethargic and even more quiet than usual. "Maybe, this is serious," I contemplated. I quickly blew off the feeling and reverted back to a teenage boy.

We drove up to Wetumka General Hospital around 11 a.m. It is still amazing to me that Wetumka had any hospital at all, but it did. My grandma and I walked through the front doors and went directly to the registration table. Directly behind the registration table was the ICU. I could see Grandpa through the glass windows. It was hard to see the strongest, most manly man I ever knew in a thin, white hospital gown laying on a bed with weird looking machines attached to him. I realized that this was no routine hospital visit: this was bad. I could feel the ice-cold fire burning in my chest again, just like I did when I saw my mom for the last time in San Francisco.

Quickly, I walked directly into the room where my grandpa was. The moment that I went through the doors and made eye contact with him, he began to breathe very heavily. In a split second, he went from looking at me to looking at the ceiling. His eyes were open, but it felt like he wasn't there. I could see stark panic in his eyes as he began to breathe like he was totally out of control. At that moment, my grandpa was in another place, another dimension. The eyes told me what was going on; my grandpa was looking at the other side.

I screamed at the top of my 14-year-old lungs, "Help! Get in here! Help!" In about 20 seconds, the nurse came in and I was escorted out of the room. It was like a really bad dream. I felt like I was having an out-of-body experience and everything started moving in agonizingly slow motion. That's why it felt like a dream. Even though I could hear all of the medical team talking, my grandma crying, and people trying to give me directions, my internal processes were moving at a snail's pace. I was lost in time and felt helpless.

They pulled the drapes across the big translucent glass wall and began to try and revive my grandpa. The doctor was not there, but they quickly called him back to the hospital. We were all in shock. People from the church suddenly started appearing. I remember Bill Cunningham showing up. He was a man's man and my grandpa's good friend. I went outside with Bill for awhile. We did some small talk and he did a good job trying to reassure me that my grandpa was going to be okay. I remember a very sweet nurse, who had been a student of "Mr. Ragland," coming out to tell us that my grandpa was going to be okay.

We were all comforted to hear that grandpa was going to be all right. I remember smiles and sighs of relief. Then about three minutes later, the same nurse came back to us crying. I knew what had happened from her face. She said with a trembling voice, "Oh Joel, I am so sorry. We lost Mr. Ragland. He had another heart attack."

Mr. Ragland, my grandpa, was dead.

I ran back down to see Grandma. She was in the lobby weeping. I ran into the ICU and saw my grandpa with his head tilted to one side and his eyes barely open. He really was gone. I wanted him to get up out of bed and take me to the Dairy Queen or to get up and watch me shoot 100 free-throws like he taught me to. But he would never move again.

"Where is Joel? I want Joel," my grandma cried.

My heart filled with anger, and I had to be alone. I ran down to the bathroom and looked in the mirror. "God, how could you do this to me?" I shouted. "I go to church, I read my Bible, and you let my mom die and now my grandpa? How could you?"

Later that night, it was just me and Grandma in the house. They had been married for 59 years. 59 years! Now she was alone. Well, almost alone. She had me, and I had her. We had one of the best talks we ever had that night. We shared sweet memories of how he was. His silent leadership. His gentle and fair way. What I really wanted to know from Grandma was if Grandpa really loved me. She told me that he loved me more than I could ever understand. We talked about an alcoholic named Higgie Hargo who Grandpa would bail out of the city jail to come work on our acreage. We talked about the time he ran down to Dead Man's Curve and pulled three teenagers out of a burning wreck. Only 2 survived. I reminisced about how he let me ride on his lap while he mowed our property with the ominous red tractor. I wore his cowboy hat and it swallowed my small, little kid head. He really was a great man.

I will never get over my grandpa. I refuse to get over him. How I wish he was here to see my kids and meet Valerie. I know he would love them, and I think he would be proud of me. I would give up every cent I have for 30 minutes with my Grandpa. Just to talk with him again, hug him, and tell him what a difference he made in my life.

Hospitals reveal the reality of life. They show how unfair life can really be. Inside of hospitals people question the goodness of God. They are confronted with the brevity of life and the meaningless of material pursuits. It really doesn't matter how big your house is if you can't breathe. Your bank account becomes irrelevant when you are filled with searing and unbearable pain. Maybe that is why I don't like hospitals. They show me how pathetic my values really are. They make me confront my mortality.

Psalm 39:4 "Show me, O Lord, my life's end and the number of my days; let me know how fleeting is my life."

My grandpa had a good life. He ended it strong, close to Christ, and with plenty of hope because of what Jesus did for him on the cross. He was ready for eternity. If we really believe in eternity, then why don't we keep it close before us? Why don't we keep reminding ourselves that we could be gone tomorrow? We lack urgency. We lack priority. We really think that our possessions make us more important. I know that I melt into that lie way too often.

When I think about our culture, I think about Donald Trump. Let's face it, in the world's eyes, he has it all. If he made $32,000 a year, we would call him a chump. But because he is rich and famous, he is honored and even respected. Well, at least in certain circles. So what do we do? We see Donald Trump and go, "If he can do it, why can't I?" And we begin the race of vanity. What will happen to Donald Trump when he dies? What will his money be worth to him?

I love Jesus. Why do I love Him? Well, one reason is because he was brutally honest. The Jesus that the American culture sees is not the Jesus of the Bible. Jesus talked about mortality considerably. Listen to this:

> **Luke 12:17-21 "The ground of a certain rich man produced a good crop. He thought to himself, 'What shall I do? I have no place to store my crops.' Then he said, 'This is what I'll do. I will tear down my barns and build bigger ones, and there I will store all my grain and my goods. And I'll say to myself, "You have plenty of good things laid up for many years. Take life easy; eat, drink, and be merry."' But God said to him, 'You fool! This very night your life will be demanded from you. Then who will get what you have prepared for yourself?' This is how it will be with anyone who stores up things for himself but is not rich toward God."**

Hospitals show us what fools we really are. They are a reminder that our hope and dependency needs to rest in God who is immutable and eternal. I still don't like hospitals, but in the end, I will probably spend my last day in one. And my prayer is that the day will be one of thanksgiving, peace, and hopeful expectations.

9

WISHING FOR THE MOON

Boom!

"What . . . was that?" I said out loud at 2:00 in the morning. At first I thought it was a dream, but then I remembered, "It must be Grandma!" I threw my covers up in the air and slid out of my bed in a panic. It was dark in the house, but I ran and dodged furniture like only a 14-year-old can.

As I entered Grandma's room in the center of the house, I could see that she was not in her bed. I quickly moved to my left and found her on the floor. This was not the first time I'd found Grandma on the floor in the middle of the night. I ran over to her and knelt down.

"Grandma! Grandma! Are you okay?" I whispered with alarm.

"Huh? Ooooh. Ooooh," she replied in confusion. The ambulance came that night, and I stayed over at the McGee's for a few days.

The doctor told us that Grandma's medicine was causing her to black out when she stood up suddenly—like in the middle of the night while she was going to the bathroom. The reason Grandma's fall that night sounded like a detonation was because our house was built on cinder blocks. For years after that, every time I heard a sonic boom, the air brakes of a bus, or some loud clamor, my heart jumped and I would lose my breath, my body involuntarily flashing back to those terrifying nighttime episodes with Grandma.

Grandma couldn't drive anymore so I had to bum rides off my friends who could drive or from Mrs. McGee from across the street. Mr. Wilkerson took me to church every Sunday morning and Wednesday night. Sometimes my algebra teacher, Mr. Tooley, would take me to church or some event.

Grandma's world-class cooking was reduced to homemade TV dinners. She no longer made pancakes in the shape of animals or Grandpa. She wasn't the same. She said it was her nerves, but in looking back, I think it was the trauma of losing her soul mate of 59 years.

My nerves were shot as well. It was hard after Grandpa's death. I blamed myself for his death—I still do sometimes. I caused him so much grief and pain. Usually it was because of my disobedience to my Grandma. I screamed at him and made him angry. Have you ever seen a Barbara Walters celebrity interview? Many times she will ask them if they have any regrets in life. I don't think I have ever heard one of them say, "Yes, I have many regrets." They always brazenly reply, "No, I wouldn't change anything." They are lying, or at least deluded. Who wouldn't want to change things they have said or done? I wish I could go back in time and tell my grandpa and grandma how sorry I am for the things I said and did. I know they are in heaven and they understand and forgive, but I still wish I had a time machine.

It wasn't all bad, though, because I'd discovered music and drama. Everybody always asks me how I got into music. My answer is two words: Lisa Fields. She was a senior, and I was in seventh grade—I thought there was a chance. There wasn't. I got involved with youth choir because Lisa was the prominent vocalist. I sang my first solo in eighth grade and was blown away by the applause from the congregation at First Baptist. People complimented me for weeks. I had found my calling.

Drama was huge for me as well. Mrs. McGee from across the street was our drama teacher. I had played the lead role in a play my seventh grade year, and I decided to audition for "The Sound of Music." I didn't get the lead role because I looked like a pip-squeak, but I did get the juicy role of Herr Zeller, the Nazi guy. I had sixteen lines and had to put white shoe polish in my hair to look like an old man. I worked on my German accent and took home the Oscar. Okay, it wasn't the Oscar, but I got the "Best Actor" award. To me, it was better than getting a real Oscar. I am still waiting for the right script for my big screen debut. Russell Crowe, look out.

But at home, things were deteriorating very quickly. A few months before, my Uncle Jim and Aunt Leola came home for Grandpa's funeral. They were missionaries in Beirut, Lebanon. They really wanted to take me in when my mom died, but my Grandma would have none of that—there was too much fighting and danger in Beirut. My uncle Jim told me that if things became too hard with Grandma, I could call the Baptist Children's Home in Oklahoma City. Things were bad, but not that bad. At least I tried to make myself believe that.

Did you ever see "The Little Rascals" on TV? The show followed the exploits of a gang of orphans—Spanky, Alfalfa, Buckwheat, and my childhood crush, Darla. I remember one episode where Spanky and the gang were at an orphanage. The superintendent of the orphanage was a skinny old man with a mustache, and he was mean.

He would chase the kids around the dilapidated, colorless orphanage with a stick! Poor Darla. An orphanage was one place that I never wanted to go.

Sometimes you don't get what you want. I was wishing for the moon. I wanted my mom and grandpa to come back, but they were gone forever from this earth. My grandma just couldn't keep on taking care of me. She would have, but I couldn't let her. At age fourteen-and-a-half, I called the Baptist Children's Home and asked to speak with a social worker. I spoke with Terri Kiefner. She was nice, and we talked for awhile. We both decided it would be good for her to come out to Wetumka and meet. When she arrived, I was distant and skeptical. She was warm and very understanding.

I loved my grandma, and I didn't want to leave her alone. Part of me felt like I betrayed her in her time of need. Part of me knew that by staying there, I was contributing to her stress, even though she would never admit that. She tried to protect me for the sake of my mother's memory. She tried to protect me because she loved me. But there was nobody left to protect her.

I made the decision to go to the Children's Home in Moore, Oklahoma. It was brand new and had moved a few miles south from Oklahoma City. Of course, I didn't care how great they said it was. In my mind, it was an old, beat-up, white house that had a skinny old man with a mustache chasing the kids with a stick!

Bill Wilkerson drove me to the Children's Home. It was a long drive, but I was so glad that Bill was with me. He was family to me. I know it was hard for him to see me go. I really do think he would have taken me in, but I would never allow myself to be a burden on him. As we entered into Moore, I remember driving down a dirt road. There was a huge blue water tower on the right side of the road.

"Where in the world are we going?," I thought to myself as we approached the campus. I don't know if I have ever felt more alone than pulling up to the Baptist Children's Home with no family, no friends, and nowhere else to go. I resolved in my mind that I needed to do what I needed to in order to survive.

There was no shabby white house. There was no skinny, mean old man chasing the kids around with a stick. We advanced towards a beautiful, state-of-the-art campus with eight stone-covered houses and an impressive gym. I began to think that maybe it wasn't such a bad move after all. Then I thought about Grandma. What was going to happen to her? I felt like I had abandoned her.

We met Mr. Browning, the superintendent of the Children's Home. His gray, wavy hair and his lanky frame were grandfatherly, and he was nice. He wore a suit and tie and he gave me some words of encouragement. What really encouraged me, though, where two things: the tone of his voice and the loving, unchanging smile on his face. I had just made my first friend at the Children's home and he was the head guy!

Bill prayed for me before saying goodbye. As his pure, Oklahoman accent reached the throne of heaven, I was sad to think of Bill leaving. He bent down to hug me, and I held on tightly, hoping that something could change, that I could go back in time or that maybe he would stay longer. I remember seeing his blue suburban drive away, and I was scared. The fear was lodged deep inside me, but I refused to show it on the outside. Instead, I went into survival mode.

I had no idea what God was doing or what was happening. Now, I see His intervening hand at almost every stage of my childhood. You might be thinking, "Joel, how could you ever love a God who allowed you to go through all of that pain and suffering?"

The love of God outweighs all of the heartache of this world. He may have allowed me to lose a lot, but He has replaced the losses with Himself. That is like trading a gum wrapper for a Lear jet. He is my gift. He is my life. As long as He is near me, I can survive and overcome anything this world can throw at me. He is that real and that good. Geraldo Rivera once said, "If something sounds too good to be true, it's not." Geraldo must have never met Christ, the Son of God. God really has turned the bad into good. Yes, there still is pain from the past in my life. It will always be there. But even that pain pushes me to the depths of His love.

God is my greatest hope. He willingly sent His precious Son, Jesus Christ, from heaven to earth to die a horrible death on the cross, to rescue me from sin and death. Even when I was all alone in this world and rejected by most, one way or another, Christ came to me. Now He is in my heart. His love is enduring and powerful. With God in my life, I can still wish for the moon.

Romans 8:38-39 "For I am persuaded that neither death nor life, nor angels nor rulers, nor things present, nor things to come, nor powers, nor height, nor depth, nor any other created thing will have the power to separate us from the love of God that is in Christ Jesus our Lord!"

10

PANCAKES AND COCA-COLA PANTS

As a kid in San Francisco, I was a mini conman. I would go down to the YMCA to find mothers who looked pretty nice, and I would tell them a sad story about being lost and needing money to get home. It worked out well for awhile, and I thought I was pretty smart. On good days, I could make six dollars in an hour. The con-job came to an end when I accidentally asked the same mother for money twice in a thirty minute run. "You are a little wheeler-dealer!" she said with a flustered disbelief.

I conned a lot of people, but most of all I conned myself. I have always been a natural communicator and thinker. I created a persona at an early age, but it wasn't really me. I had no idea who I was. I wanted to be Captain Kirk or a pro wrestler. Not having a dad left me without an identity. In my grandparents' eyes, I was the sweet, perfect grandchild. At school, I was the troubled, hyperactive boy without a dad. At home with my mom I had been the funny, needy, and angry son. But inside myself I felt like I was none of those people. I was lost.

When I moved to Wetumka, I was picked on almost every day. Being a skinny, highly extroverted kid with a temper probably didn't help me. Somewhere around eighth grade, I decided I'd had enough of the bullying. I would never tolerate disrespect again. I made it clear that if you messed with me, you would definitely get in a fight. Sometimes that made it worse, and other times it intimidated would-be bullies. I remember getting in an all-out fistfight with one of the Yahola brothers at the football stadium one night. It was a close fight, and it helped cement my reputation as a kid who was willing to stand up for himself if he had to. I did not have an imposing stature, so I had to make up for it with my trash-talking rhetoric and scrappy attitude to back it up. It was another persona—another con.

Moving to the Children's home in Moore was a new start for me. I had a clean slate, and I was going to get as much mileage out of it as possible. I had become a good student and was very clean cut. Somehow, by the grace of God, I had avoided stealing, drinking, drugs, and other teenage pitfalls. I had a great image at the Children's Home, and I wasn't going to blow it.

The Baptist Children's home was a state-of-the-art facility in its day. I remember there there were eight large, single-story houses as well as a brand new gym and swimming pool with a retractable roof. The houses were called "cottages" for some reason, but they were much larger than what I thought of as a "cottage." Each cottage had a married couple who were called house parents. House parents were fulltime staff that lived in the houses. They were on call 24 hours a day with one day off each week. That's when an "associate house parent" came in for the day. During the summers, all the boys at the home were put on the grounds crew or what I called the "work detail." We also did house chores every day.

My first house parents were Mr. and Mrs. Green at Memorial Cottage. I am sure they are not as bad as I thought they were back then, but I was not used to the strict structure of "Home" life. Looking back, I can only imagine how hard it must have been to be a houseparent at a Children's Home. I am sure it was hard on their marriage, their son Greg, and their finances. Dealing with eight troubled kids on top of your own family can only be tough. I walked the line pretty tightly, and we got along well.

I got along with my first roommate, Seth. His full name was Seth Tiffany, which I always thought was a cool name. Seth was a very friendly guy, who knew the "ropes" about how to survive at the "Home." We immediately got along and we made each other laugh. He left about a month after I arrived, and my next roommate was a nightmare. The new guy eventually moved across the hall, and my next roommate was even worse. Of course, I didn't let the Greens know that I hated living in their house. I didn't want to blow it at the Home. Where else would I go if I made trouble?

That mentality of "not blowing it" has haunted me all of my life.

Like I told you before, I was a wheeler-dealer. I did some backroom negotiating and was transferred to a "cottage" that I thought would be more appropriate for me. Tim and Susan Rogers were the coolest house parents on campus. They lived in Kerr Cottage and, three months into my stay, I moved into Kerr. Tim was a former youth pastor and was funny, loving, smart, and a great musician. He and I hit it off big time. He even had these pants that were made of polyester and had the Coke brand all over them. They looked hilarious on him! How can you not love a guy who is willing to wear Coca-Cola pants! Tim could play the piano, and we sang songs together every day. My favorite song that Tim would sing was "Hey Man, Do You Know My Lord?" It was a reggae-tinged song that was a big hit in the early 70's. He would sing it and play the piano standing up, totally getting into it! He was a true joy to be around.

Tim and Susan were passionate about Jesus Christ. We studied the Bible together, and I loved their two kids, Bryan and Kenny. Yes, they had a son named Kenny Rogers. There were many moments of fun and laughter in the home, like the time Kenny fell asleep at the table and used his plate full of food as a pillow.

Some of my favorite people that came to visit us were the Engles. The Engles were best friends with Tim and Susan. Dale Engle was a thin, kind of quiet man who wore a ball cap all the time. I remember Tim telling me that Dale Engle was the finest man he'd ever met. That caught me off guard because I thought Tim was the finest person I'd ever met. Nadine Engle was Dale's wife. She was very funny and had a sweet toughness about her. She could take a joke and give it back to you in a flash. I liked her a lot, but I would never mess with her.

I *would* mess with my housemates, though. As I tried out my new persona at the Home, I practiced talking smack. I think I picked it up from all the pro wrestling I watched. One day I was talking about how much I could eat. At the Home, all of the food was served on the table, and whoever ate the fastest received the most food. There was only the food that was put on the table, so we had to pack it away fast. During our morning breakfast chitchat, I told everybody that I could eat 20 pancakes in one sitting. I was just blowing smoke, but Tim and Susan remembered my words. About three weeks later, I came to the breakfast table. Everybody was watching me. I thought that some of my bad deeds had caught up to me or that I had blown it.

Tim came out and said, "Joel, remember when you said you could eat 20 pancakes in one sitting?"

I replied in the macho-pubescent manner of a fifteen-year-old, "Yeah, that would be easy."

All of the sudden, a tray of 20 pancakes came out from the kitchen. I was stunned. Somebody had called me out. I had one of two choices: humiliation or pain. I chose pain. Four glasses of milk, two bottles of syrup, and thirteen napkins later, I ate the last pancake. Then I went on work detail, mowing what seemed to be 200 acres of grass. After eating those pancakes, I thought I mowed the whole state of Oklahoma! Let's just say that eating 20 pancakes and doing manual labor in the wicked Oklahoma heat was not a pretty sight for my fellow "home-kids" that had to work with me that day.

There were eight kids in our cottage. Wally was about 12. He was very angry and had to go see the psychologist each week. I didn't get to go see Dr. Mcallie, but I probably should have. Tien Van Chow was my roommate. He was nine and from Vietnam. He and his two brothers came to America as refugees. Tien was the cutest kid I have ever seen. He was hilarious, but he had a temper the size of Vietnam. I made the mistake of making him very angry one day, and he began to catapult these huge Tonka toys (made of die-cast metal with very pointy edges) at me. I locked myself in the bathroom, and I watched the Tonka toys puncture the brown bathroom door as they hit the other side with the force of Tien's fury behind them. Tim came in and saved me that day.

Roger Hull was my roommate a few months before Tien. He was a compulsive liar, but he could tell some stories! He was really smart, and he knew it. He definitely surpassed me as the new wheeler-dealer on campus.

I remember little Stormie and her big sister Kerri. They were sad little girls. They didn't deserve the pain that they carried around inside. None of those kids did. They were innocent children who absorbed the mistakes and sins of their parents. Selfishness destroys those around us. Nobody can say, "I am not hurting anybody, just myself." Divorce, drugs, alcoholism, rage; the resulting collateral damage is staggering. I am glad I got a good dose of human reality early-on in my life. I think it helped me realize what is important, and it gave me the ability to sift out the real from the fake, the truth from the bull.

There is so much futility in this world. I have been caught up in it way too much in my lifetime. People are always chasing something, whether it's sex, money, pleasure, or any other futile dead end or red herring. I will never forget what football great Tom Brady said in an interview on the show "60 Minutes." With movie star good looks, fame, tons of money, and amazing opportunities at his fingertips, he said, "I thought there would be more." Astounding. That is what happens when you get older. You think, "Is that it? Isn't there something more than just making money, having a decent house, and collecting things?"

I tried to be so many things. I even tried to be myself. Still, all I found was emptiness. It kind of reminds me of the woman at the well in the Bible. She came to the same watering hole every day, but her thirst was never entirely quenched. Then she met Jesus and He said " . . .whoever **drinks from the water that I will give him will never get thirsty again—ever!" (John 4:14)** She thought physically, but Jesus meant "spiritually." We are thirsty souls, aren't we? Lapping up every relationship we can, but never completely satisfied. Gulping in as much "entertainment" we can, only to be bored twenty minutes later. Sipping at religion only to feel the bewilderment of emptiness.

The person—the historical, existent person of Jesus Christ—is the only thing that relieves the silent ache in the vacuum of our inner beings. Humanity is constantly reaching outside only to bring back hands that are empty. We must realize that we are not machines but souls, spiritual creatures that are either infused with the life of Christ or confused at the meaninglessness of existence.

I hunger. Not for pancakes, but for meaning. A Rolls Royce is no different than a pancake. You get really, really full and then the next day you are hungry again. It is a perpetual vicious cycle. I hunger. Not for instant delight but for substance; something that will last. Jesus Christ said, "**I have food to eat that you don't know about**" (John 4:32). Even Christians don't know about it. Half the time, I forget about this food for the soul. I snack on the raw ideology of American life and feel sick. It feels like eating too much candy—at first I am full but then my stomach starts to hurt. For the believer in Jesus Christ, we have access to food that really does satisfy. It is as available as McDonald's but without the looming heart attack. Jesus said, "**I am the bread of life . . . no one who comes to Me will ever be hungry**" (John 6:35). Why don't I go to Jesus more often when I hunger? Because I am a fool. I get conned by the world and by Satan. I get conned by myself.

Last night, I was hungry and I came to Jesus. He really does satisfy. This morning I woke up and I wanted more—more of Him. Not more of theology or more songs to record or more anecdotes to spew—I wanted more of Him. I am tired of being a sucker, aren't you?

"Nothing so defiles and entangles the heart of man as the impure love of creatures. If you refuse to be comforted from without, you will be able to contemplate the things of heaven, and often to rejoice within."

—*Thomas a Kempis*

11

KEITH GREEN AND GARBER, OKLAHOMA

Music is emotion translated into sound. That's how I explain music to nonmusical people. When the notes are played or sung with the right dynamics and chordal structure, they hit you in the soul. That is why I have always loved Marvin Gaye, who is most famous for singing "I Heard It Through the Grapevine." My favorite song of his is "What's Going On?" There is pathos in his music that stirs my heart. He sang with pain, and it was messy. It was real.

For me, the greatest Christian musician of all time, without question, was Keith Green. If you have never heard of Keith Green, it is because he died in a tragic plane wreck at the age of 28. I discovered Keith Green in the seventh or eighth grade on the radio. He put the Bible, real life experiences, and passionate, unrelenting music together in a way that changed my life. He didn't care what people thought, either. He challenged the church to stop being so apathetic about God and lost people. He took people off the street and let them live in his home. He wasn't a talker but a doer. He was real. I could identify with his personal struggles as a Christian. He introduced me to a way of feeling that I had never experienced. Vulnerability.

Openness. Worship. His songs were God-centered and filled with humble theology. Christian music needs to get back to that, and fast.

Tim and Susan played a lot of Keith Green in the cottage. I remember waking up and walking past the house stereo circa 1984. I would hear songs like "There Is A Redeemer" or "I Can't Believe," and my heart would immediately soar into the arms of Christ.

I probably became a Christian in the eighth grade. I was at Falls Creek again, and I actually tracked down Dr. Jim Henry, the camp pastor that week, to ask him to lead me to Christ. I was crazy like that. I still am. Dr. Henry was shocked and appeared slightly agitated when I asked him if I could come into his hotel room to talk. I got right down to business and told him that I knew I was not a Christian. There was a knock at the door and a man was on the other side, waiting to take Dr. Henry golfing. Dr. Henry whispered something, and the man took off for the fairways. I am glad that Dr. Henry didn't go golfing that day. He really warmed up to me when he figured out how shaken up I was about my eternal destiny. He kindly and lovingly explained to me how Jesus died for me. I understood what he was talking about, and I sincerely asked Christ to come into my life. That was when Jesus saved my life with the blood he shed on the cross. But the doubts followed me.

In 1984, I turned 16 and came down with the chicken pox. Sixteen-year-old kids don't need the chicken pox. It is like having really bad acne—that's on fire. I was miserable. I was quarantined in my room for two weeks. I couldn't see anyone, and only Susan Rogers was allowed to see me. The only book that I had in my room was my Bible. I had some textbooks from school, but I had a decent excuse not to do homework, so I wasn't about to crack one open. Instead, I read my Bible and began to question whether or not I was truly a Christian. I did this secretly because I was afraid of what people would think of me. I was a leader at the Children's Home and in my youth group. I was the strong Christian that everybody came to when they had questions about the Bible. My image was in danger. Yet the doubts kept growing, and the fear kept swelling up inside of me. How could I have been a Christian and punched out my Grandpa? Or left my Grandma "out in the cold" (or so my emotions kept haunting me)? Or lusted? Or hated? The questions kept growing, and my faith kept shrinking.

My relationship with the Engles was developing as well. During holidays, the Children's Home campus would shut down and the residents (kids) would either go home or be placed in sponsor homes. Sponsor homes were families across the state who would take you in for a few days during the holidays. The worst place to be on earth is with strangers during the holidays. Holidays are for family, not for strangers.

During fall break of 1984, I went to stay with the Engles. They were not strangers. Even if I had just met them, they wouldn't have been strangers. They were like Keith Green to me. Open and real. All of my weirdness, hurt, humor, and past were completely welcomed in their home. To this day, I have never met people who welcomed in strangers into their home like the Engle's. I tried to be on my best behavior so I wouldn't do anything to make them not like me.

The family consisted of Mr. and Mrs. Engle and their children: Eva Jo, Mary Ruth, Gregg, and Nancy. Gregg and Nancy were older and didn't live at home. Eva Jo was something else. She was a true "free-spirit", a natural leader and super fun. She was a year older than me. She acted like she knew me, and we hit it off. Mary Ruth was my age and very nice. They were cool. I tried to make sure they thought I was cool, too. I didn't know if they could see through my forced persona or not because they were so over the top nice.

Being at the Engles for fall break was like a little slice of heaven. They had a 20 year-old son named Gregg who was a college student at Oklahoma Baptist University. His clothes were all ripped up, and he was a musician. He was a singer and a bass player, and could even play the piano. The best part about Gregg was that he actually talked to me. That was cool.

I didn't want fall break to end. The question that kept running through my mind was, "Maybe the Engles will adopt me." I was hoping for a miracle. I could never ask them, though. You don't ask people if you can live with them—they might say no. I began to pray to God that he would make the Engles want to adopt me.

At Moore West Middle School, I was not cool and I was definitely not myself. I wanted to be "normal" and was deeply embarrassed to be living in a Children's Home. Some kids treated me differently because I lived in an "orphanage," but most of the kids didn't know where I lived. The insecurity of being made fun of, looked down on, and being an outcast seemed to paralyze my outgoing personality. I didn't talk much and I kept to myself so I didn't draw attention to my status as an orphan.

My clothes were certainly not cool. I remember one time in choir when a football player decided to make fun of my "terry cloth" shirt. I loved that shirt. My grandma bought it for me, and it reminded me of her. I didn't know it was about four years out of style. I didn't care, either. When the football player kept at it, I exploded and jumped out of my chair. I don't remember what I said, but the teasing permanently stopped. I hated school.

Weeks passed on by. I forgot about the Engles and my prayer. I was not a beggar, and I could manage on my own. I got home from school one day and there was a memo for me from Teri Kiefner, my social worker. You only went to see your social worker when you really messed up. I had done all kinds of things under the radar of the Children's Home, but I thought that I had covered my tracks pretty well. When I was a kid, I was paranoid about everything. I lived under the burden of questions like, "What deceitful act will be my final undoing?" More than a few things raced through my mind as I walked over to the main office from Kerr cottage.

I sat down in Teri's office in the chair facing her desk. "Joel, something interesting has developed," she said in a cryptic manner.

I immediately thought about what I did at the swimming pool the previous week. I had picked on some kid and held him underwater, threatening to give him a serious beat-down if he told on me. "No, that can't be it," I thought to myself as my pulse slightly increased.

"Well, Joel, the Engle family has made a request. They want to be a foster home to you."

I was taken aback. I had not expected my prayers to be answered. Surreal is a great word to describe how I felt at that moment. You know how you can be so overjoyed and thankful that you want to cry? It really is an ironic feeling. I held back the tears and realized that it was about thirty seconds since she told me the news. I quickly responded "Uh . . . yeah, I . . . They want me? . . .To live with them?"

Teri smiled with subdued joy. "Yes, Joel, they want you."

Contrary to popular belief, there are trees in Garber, Oklahoma. It just doesn't look like it when you are driving into the town. Garber is a really small town. It is a farming community made up of mostly white, lower-income people. People from Garber are not overly warm when you meet them, except for the Engles. People from Garber are smart but simple, distant but polite.

Driving up I-35 from Oklahoma City, I could see the traces of winter as the snowy ice streaked the flatlands. The fence posts danced past my view as we drifted towards my new home. I thought about Tim, Susan, and Grandma. I thought about the kids that I would leave at the Home who had no place to go. I felt a little guilty. I didn't understand why I was able to have a new home while they had to remain orphans. Those thoughts evaporated as I mused about what life would be like in Garber.

Life is like music. It soars up and down, flowing from happiness to despair. Good music is unpredictable, just like life. Music was meant to express beauty. Even though life is often not beautiful, it was created for beauty. Walking into the house at Garber was beautiful. You would not be that impressed with the house, but the people were beautiful because of the song that was inside of them.

The life of Moses was like a majestic opera. He lived in the minor key of danger, death, disappointment, and failure. He also walked in the passion and presence of God and spoke with God as one speaks with a friend. God was his song. I can agree with Moses that the beauty of the song of my life is Jesus Christ. Through the soaring peaks and lonely valleys, His melody of love has carried me along.

Exodus 15:2 "The LORD is my strength and my song; He has become my salvation. This is my God, and I will praise Him, my father's God, and I will exalt Him."

12

NOT BLOWING IT

L ife in Garber, Oklahoma was slow—really slow. People drove, walked, talked, and ate as if they were covered in molasses. I needed to slow down because I had been running for a long time. Running from my fears and doubts. Running from my shame and guilt. I didn't trust people. I knew how to smile, joke around, and wheel and deal, but it was tiresome. I was way too tired for a sixteen year-old kid.

When you live in an establishment like the Children's Home, you become institutionalized. The culture of a Children's Home thrives on structure and routine. I did the exact same thing every day. I woke up, made my bed, took a shower, did my chores, ate breakfast, waited for the school bus, etc. Kids who come out of chaos need order, and they need it bad. There were rules. We were not allowed to answer the phone. We couldn't get anything out of the refrigerator. We couldn't go outside without permission. And so on.

Life with the Engles was very different than the Home. I was a free man, I just didn't know it. For several days, I would come home and just sit in a chair because I didn't know what to do. The phone would ring and I would be frozen in fear. Everybody wondered why I didn't answer the phone. They didn't realize that I was just obeying the rules.

I would sit in the chair, hungry and thirsty. I would ask Mrs. Engle (I call her Mom now, and will call her Mom for the rest of the book) if I could have a drink. She would stare at me and say with an incredulous tone, "Of course, Joel, you are a member of our family." The next day, I would ask again. This would be repeated day after day.

One day, Mom finally came to me in my chair and said, "Joel, this is your home. You can answer the phone anytime you want to, and you can get a snack or a Coke from the fridge whenever you want."

I'm reminded of a scene in the movie *The Shawshank Redemption* where Red (played by Morgan Freeman) was working in a grocery store. Red had just been released from prison, where he had spent most of his life. He would constantly say to the store manager, "Bathroom-break boss?" The manager told him he didn't have to ask anymore. I can relate to that. Freedom is a weird thing when you have been without it for awhile.

The next day Mom came into the house and was surprised to see me sitting in my chair again. The only difference was that I was on the phone, and Coke cans and scattered bags of chips covered the floor. Sometimes freedom is hard to accept, and at the same time, hard to handle.

Before moving in with the Engles, I struggled with feeling like people underestimated me, so I spent much of my life trying to prove people wrong. But when someone you respect believes in you, it goes a long, long way. There is power when someone believes in you, and Mom and Dad Engle believed in me. Dad is not a big talker, but he is secretly sentimental—you can feel it when he is sentimental about you.

Mom is all out in the open, and she is not that sentimental. She went through unimaginable pain as a child, and she doesn't allow self-pity in her presence. At that age, I agreed with George Constanza's philosophy that "pity is very underrated." I don't think Mom Engle and George Constanza would have seen eye-to-eye. The Engles didn't allow me to wallow in pity. They showed me that I was a person of value and great potential. They actually seemed to respect me, and they showed me the love of God.

I had no self-confidence at all. That is probably why I bragged so much—I was trying to feel powerful. A few years ago, I spoke at a Children's Home in South Texas. I was invited to eat dinner at a cottage before I spoke, and I was intrigued by the table talk. Several of the young men at the table were serious "trash talkers." When your life is ripped out from under your feet, you want to find a way to control your environment around you so that it doesn't happen again. Bragging is a way to make yourself feel powerful when in reality, you feel weak. Rappers are a great example of this.

Even in the midst of my trash talking, the Engles helped me see that I was lovable. This was displayed in an event of monumental proportions. I played basketball in high school. I was okay, but God gave me the body of a piano player—not an athlete. I had the heart of a champion, but the physique of spaghetti. The very first day of practice we were doing lay up drills on the court when I accidentally bumped the kid in front of me. Words and threats were exchanged. When I got back to the locker room, punches were also exchanged. Our locker room was covered with red carpet and at one point the fight went to the ground. Both of us had world-class carpet burns on our faces, elbows, and knees. We were real smart.

When the fight was over I was in a panic. I had only been at Garber High School for one week, and I was certain I would be suspended when Coach Dell found out about my altercation. My track record of "not blowing it" was about to come to a brutal end. I began to make preparations in my mind. I couldn't hide behind the smile and the jokes anymore. When you don't feel lovable, you are hard to love. It's a sad pattern that develops. My first thought was to reject the Engles before they rejected me.

I walked into the house and saw my new friend of about one month, Robert Campbell, sitting in Dad's chair. Robert was a tall, thin, and super-smart senior with black glasses who befriended me the first day I arrived. He greeted me as I walked through the living room. I responded, "Shut your face and leave me alone." Slamming the door, I sat on the edge of my bed, staring at the closet. I looked down at my luggage that was on the bottom of my closet floor. My burgundy, well-worn bags looked as dejected as I felt. I didn't want to leave the Engles, but I couldn't face the rejection that I thought was waiting to pounce on me.

Mom walked into my room and reprimanded me for the way that I spoke to Robert. I knew she was right, but I tried to keep up a tough exterior.

"What is the matter, Joel? Why are you acting this way?" Mom asked, her voice hard, yet loving.

"When I tell you what I did today, you are not going to want me around anymore." I replied.

I began to tell her about the fight and what I thought the consequences would be for me at school. "You don't know me and you don't love me so I want to go back to the Children's home," I said, knowing that I was lying through my teeth.

Sometimes peoples' responses are not what you expect. What Mom said to me that night changed everything.

"Joel, I want you to listen to me. No matter how bad you are or how good you are, we will always love you, and you will always have a home here with us."

I couldn't believe she said that. Grace. When I forget what grace is, I go back to that statement. Grace is being loved by someone for no other reason except that they want to love you. That night, a lot of walls came down—or at least the process of demolition began.

Up to that point in my life, I had felt like a "fifth-wheel"—like I was always on the outside looking in. I walked on the egg shells of "not blowing it" so I could keep being loved, or at least accepted. For the first time I felt like I could maybe trust Mom and Dad. A few nights later, I had a talk with Mom concerning my fear of not being a Christian. We agreed that this was a matter that needed to be resolved.

The First Baptist Church of Garber, Oklahoma was not a mega-church. It was a tiny-church. There were some great people in that church like Mrs. Kime, Roy Cogden, and Preacher Gilmore (who wasn't actually a preacher, he just had the nickname). What made them great was the fact that they were older than me but still loved me and were wonderfully warm to me every time I met them. Love and kindness are the eternal disintegrators of generational gaps.

Our pastor, Lynn Nickel, was a really good man and an excellent preacher. He took a special interest in me. I had contemplated coming to terms with the horrible doubts about whether or not I was really a Christian. I probably was a Christian, but the doubts, fears, and bad theology made it really tough on me. Plus, in the Baptist church, they really emphasize "nailing down your decision." I appreciate their motives, but sometimes a person really needs to talk things through without someone trying to get a decision out of him. Most Baptists are great evangelists, but horrible listeners. Mom was a good listener and a good evangelist.

It was a Sunday morning, and I was sitting on the back row. Usually I sat in the front, but our youth group sat in the back. As the new guy, I wanted to fit in. Pastor Nickel was out of town and a stand-in pastor named Archie Kluysmeyer was there. From what I remember of what he preached that day, it was a simple message about how Jesus died on the cross and bore the wrath of God upon Himself for us—for me. I thought of Mom telling me she would love me no matter what, and it all came together.

In my excitement, I followed the Baptist tradition of walking down the aisle at the altar-call time. Everybody conveniently forgot to tell me that nobody ever came down the aisle at Garber. You should have seen the deacon at the front of the church! He was scared out of his mind as he watched me walk closer and closer to the front where he was standing. Mom Engle stepped between us and took me off to the side. She's crazy like that. Still is.

Mom and I talked for awhile, and I was honest with God about my doubts and fears. I told Him that I accepted His grace and the gift of His Son, Jesus Christ. As far as really doubting my salvation, I haven't experienced a whole lot of that since. Usually, I just marvel at how consistently strong God's love really is. The more I have tested it, the more it holds up. God is good; even though I still get caught up in the whole "not blowing it" trap from time to time.

Walking into the Engles' house was walking into their unconditional love. It is the same with salvation. When we walk under the shadow of the cross of Christ, we walk into the shelter of His never-ending love. He takes us just as we are, in all of our weakness and fragility—even when we blow it.

1 John 3:1 "How great is the love the Father has lavished on us, that we should be called children of God! And that is what we are! The reason the world does not know us is that it did not know him."

13

FOOD COURT AND BEER

T his is going to sound weird, but I like to watch people eat—especially at the food court in the mall. I will usually focus on a person eating alone; it stirs compassion deep within me. When someone is eating by himself, the person seems so vulnerable. Almost every time, the person has a childlike expression. I guess it's because eating is a primal and basic instinct of humanity. We have to eat, or we will eventually die. I think it's also because nobody likes to eat alone, and you can see a fearful isolation and loneliness in the person's eyes. Everyone fears loneliness. Maybe that is why cell phones are so huge—because you never have to be alone . . . if you can get ahold of somebody!

I spent much of my early years alone because I was an only child. Being an only child stinks; I hated it. I always envied families. I wanted a brother or sister; instead I received a cat. Then another cat. Both of our cats ran away because of all the commotion on the day my mom died, which only added to my loneliness.

The Engle household was different. The house was always booming with people; it was the processing station for Garber teenagers. There was always someone to talk to, to laugh, to eat with. Becoming an Engle was a big deal to me because it meant that I didn't have to be alone anymore.

Dad was easygoing and almost happy-go-lucky. He would always come in from work singing his "doot-doot" song . It was a daily ritual, when dad would come home he would come hope singing the same countryish melody with the words "doot, doot, doot." That is just one of the little unique things that make Dale Engle so cool. He had a way of talking to you that made you feel special. Mom was tough but also loving and honest. If you didn't want her opinion, then you didn't ask for it. I respect people like that. She also had a temper. Now it is mostly gone, but back then you didn't want to mess with her.

I didn't fit in at Garber, except at the Engles' house. I had strong Christian beliefs by then, and I didn't drink or party. I was amazed at how many kids at Garber High School partied. There was a hopelessness surrounding the youth in Garber. I don't know if it was Garber's isolation from mainstream society or something else, but there was darkness there. When all the kids at Garber partied on Friday night, I was glad to be at home. I loved being home—I couldn't get enough of it.

I loved playing basketball, but I also loved music. Mom told me that I could either play basketball or make music, but I couldn't do both. I told her that I would rather do basketball and skip music. She told me that I was going to do music. I was so mad at her, but she was right. I had much more talent in music than I did in sports. The problem was that although I could sing well, I couldn't play an instrument. I never had the opportunity to take any kind of music lessons. I had always wanted to learn how to play the piano so I could write songs. One day in my room, I was frustrated because I wanted to write a song about what God was doing in my life. Somewhere in that moment I decided to pray to God. This was the prayer:

"Father, if you will give me the ability to play the piano, I will never sing or write a song that doesn't glorify You."

I meant that prayer with all my heart.

The Engles had a piano in Eva's room. About a week after my prayer, I sat down at that piano. I don't know what really happened that day, but as I sat down to try to play, music came out of my heart and flowed over the piano keys. It was unearthly. The song I wrote that day actually became our class song, and I sang it at my high school graduation.

This period in Garber was an important time in the formation of my music ministry. When my pastor heard me sing, he asked me to "lead the singing" at our church. This was before the advent of what people call "modern worship." I dislike that term quite a bit because worship isn't modern, it is ancient. God placed the desire for worship in the heart of humanity in the Garden of Eden. We should call "modern worship" something different like "rock and roll influenced praise music." Anyway, I "led the singing" at our church. What that entailed was me swinging my arms around, pretending to conduct the pianist and organist while I actually followed them. They were the musicians and I was the guy trying to sing.

When I look back, I really had no business being in any kind of leadership role. What I really needed was someone to invest in my life and teach me the Scriptures and how to be a man. However, through "leading the singing" at my church, people found out about my singing talent and asked me to come sing at Christian events around the area. That was the beginning of me finding my calling.

People will always tell you what they think your calling in life is. Some are accurate, but most are just clueless. My mom had some kind of inside scoop on God's will for my life—a premonition about my call to the ministry. I could feel the message of Christ burning deep inside of me, but I didn't really know how to articulate it. There was also a tension inside of me growing. I was tired of being the "fifth-wheel" at school. What I needed was an image makeover.

I decided to run for Student Council President because I was tired of being unnoticed. I had an outgoing personality and was a pretty good speaker. Intrinsically, I knew how to market myself. So I did. I had two campaign slogans and one marketing strategy. The first slogan was "Get rid of the static and vote for Joel Craddick." Looking back, it's a bit dorky, but I thought it was cool at the time. The other slogan was "Vote Joel for total control." There was a picture of the world superimposed over the slogan. Kind of scary. My wife, Valerie, will often quote that slogan to me when I get too demanding.

My marketing strategy was this: since all the kids in my class hated me (the new kid), I would win over the 9th and 10th grade girls. I flirted, joked, and went out of my way to win that important demographic, which is funny because we only had about 100 people in the whole high school. Eventually my slogans and marketing strategy paid off and I won! I can't tell you what an impact that had on my life. I discovered something about myself: I was a leader. I had drive, initiative, and organizational gifts. I had no idea that those characteristics were inside of me until I decided to run for STUCO (Student Council) president.

I did pretty well that year. STUCO actually made money for the first time, and I put on two huge events in Garber. First was the "Mister Garber" pageant. Basically, it was a beauty contest that all the Senior guys in my class participated in. It was hilarious to see these macho guys doing a "male" beauty pageant. It was a big hit and as I look back I can see the origin of some of my leadership qualities. You should have been there, you would have gotten a kick out of it. The other was some type of Luau. There was dancing involved so Mom, who was a very devout Southern Baptist, didn't approve at all. She brought up the conflict between being the "song leader" at our church (who didn't believe in dancing, card playing, and drinking . . . in that order) and putting on a dance for the entire town. Dancing could lead to card playing and total anarchy. I told her that I understood the problem, but since the Luau was happening that night, and I was the guy putting it on, canceling would bring some credibility issues into my administration (I was trying to sound very important . . . this was politics in Garber)! After awhile, Mom calmed down and told me I could attend, but to make sure I conducted myself as a Christian. I did. No dancing and no card playing.

My greatest regret in Garber was my behavior on our Senior class trip. Before then, peer pressure never fazed me. For some reason, early on in my life, I had deep convictions about certain issues. I didn't drink or party. I did have a girlfriend for a while my Senior year, but I broke up with her because she publicly disrespected her dad at Pizza Inn one night. Yet, I wanted to know what the big deal was about partying and drinking. Why were kids so enamored with getting drunk? Somewhere on the way down to Dallas (by the way, going to Dallas is like going to New York City when you live in Garber), I decided to see if getting drunk was that big of a deal.

First, it didn't take a whole lot of alcohol to get me intoxicated. I weighed about 135 pounds and had never tasted beer. Also, the beer in Texas was more intoxicating than in Oklahoma from what I heard. Secondly, beer didn't taste good to me. My mom (not Mom Engle) would let me taste wine and champagne when I was a kid during holidays in San Francisco, and it that tasted pretty decent. However, beer tasted terrible to me. Thirdly, the drinking party wasn't that fun. It was like everybody spent all their time drinking. There were no meaningful conversations or interacting, except drinking. It was just one big drinking game. I kept thinking, "This is what the big deal is? This is the reality behind all the bragging and anticipation? This is stupid." Our sponsors (two teachers from school—one a member of First Baptist) encouraged the drinking. It was just so meaningless to me, the whole thing. I did try to kiss a few girls, but my breath was probably horrible. What I did do, however, was destroy the testimony that I had built to my classmates. All the "Jesus talk" was compromised by my participation in that weekend. The next day, I was so sick that I promised myself I would never get drunk again.

I had decided to go to Oklahoma Baptist University and study music. Two days after I graduated from GHS, I moved to Shawnee, Oklahoma to get a jump start on college. I was going to start a new life and I couldn't wait for the fall. I had no patience about stuff I wanted to do. My wife will tell you, I still don't.

People are empty glasses, waiting for love to pour inside of them. I guess that is why the kids in Garber wanted to party. They didn't have to be alone, and they could drink in something that felt like love for a few hours. Some years ago, I got an invitation to my ten-year high school reunion. The card said "bring plenty of beer." The emptiness of the human heart is perpetual. It never gets satisfied. We are alone in this world whether we are married, at the food court of a mall, at a party, or president of some organization. We are alone, trapped inside of our minds, yet craving to connect with something that will quench our spiritual dehydration. That is why Christ called Himself "living water." He alone can quench the nagging thirst of our souls.

Psalm 63:1 "God, You are my God; I eagerly seek You. I thirst for You; my body faints for You in a land that is dry, desolate, and without water."

14

DOES GOD LOVE GOLF?

When I was a kid, I didn't know that golf existed. It just never appeared on my sports radar. Sometime in college, I started hearing about golf every once in awhile. Finally I was invited to play with a friend, and I was horrible—dangerously so. A few years later, some of my buddies started playing, and I learned to love it. I remember the first time I hit the golf ball well. It is kind of like hitting a homerun—you feel powerful.

The great thing about playing golf with your buddies is the mulligan, which is the golfing term for a "do over." If you hit a really bad shot, then you pull another golf ball from your pocket to try again, hoping that it doesn't go in the water, out of bounds, or into the back of somebody's head. The true rules of golf do not recognize the mulligan. That is fine because most recreational golfers don't recognize the true rules of golf. The mulligan can turn an incredibly frustrating game into a leisurely, relaxing round of golf.

For me, going to Oklahoma Baptist University was a type of mulligan—a do over. I had always hated how I came across to people my own age in high school. I had consistently felt awkward and alienated from my peers. College was freedom: freedom from the misconceptions that people had of me; freedom from the pigeonholed identity that I had all through my teenage years; freedom from the past.

I think that Mom and Dad Engle did a great job preparing me for life after graduation. Yet, nothing can totally prepare a young person for sudden, unobserved, and unbridled freedom. When I arrived at OBU that June, the campus was close to empty. There may have been two hundred students at the most. I was loving life from the very second I set foot in Shawnee.

I was able to meet people from all over Oklahoma and North Texas, especially girls. I had just discovered dating a few months earlier, and I was ready to meet as many girls as possible. But freedom is a hard car to drive if you haven't had much experience behind the wheel. I had some pretty bad wrecks that summer. Basically, I fell away from dependence upon God. Even though I had an Old Testament class and occasionally went to church, I began to cut God out of the picture of my life. It wasn't a totally conscious decision; it was more of a gradual, downward slide into sin. That's where I landed spiritually. I became colder and colder in my heart toward Christ, who had given His life to set me free from sin.

Part of my descent was that I had no clue as to who I was as a person. I was a good actor, so I created a role for myself that I thought would have some social box-office appeal. I didn't understand the call of Christ to abandon all for Him.

As a music major, I was ready to do whatever it took to make the grades and, more importantly, hone my skills as a singer, songwriter, and overall musician. When fall session began, it was extremely difficult and demanding on my time. My drive to succeed was very intense. Of course, I still had time for girls. I took out a lot of girls that semester and became somewhat popular as a freshman. That is, until the freshman girls discovered that I didn't call my dates back after a few rendezvous. My relationships with the girls at OBU were primarily innocent, but I had no idea how to treat a lady. Dating was more for my ego than anything else, and after I realized that I was a little attractive to the opposite sex, I began to feel an emptiness in my heart. My self esteem was based on my success in getting girls to go out with me, but it wasn't as fulfilling as I thought it would be. I felt distant and unknown. No one truly knew the real me, they only knew the character I portrayed in the show of trying to prove my worth as an individual.

I was in piano class one day when Jeff Coleman walked into the classroom. "Who is *this* guy?" I muttered in my mind as I hit some really bad chords due to the distraction. Mrs. Timberlake smacked my hands for that. Jeff silently took his bench in our group piano class. He was dressed in a cool sweater and had a look of determination etched onto his face.

I had sized up my competition in the music school pretty well, but I wasn't prepared for another rival. After class, I quickly introduced myself to Jeff. We really hit it off, and after a few weeks I began to think he was a cool guy. I noticed something different about Jeff because had a depth of thought and a genuine love for God that starkly contrasted the typical shallow religion that I saw on campus. My expectations of going to a "Christian" university were very naïve because I expected the majority of students to be radically passionate about God and totally into Jesus—like a four year church camp. I thought people would be praying on the grass for all the lost souls, inviting me to endless amounts of Bible studies, and singing worship songs in the cafeteria. In reality, most of the students were pretty casual in their Christianity—just like me. Jeff was nothing like us. He read his Bible with passion and wrote out his prayers to God in a journal. He was very nice and also very, very talented.

Jeff started challenging some of the things I was doing on campus. I was too scared to "go off the deep end," but I was definitely headed in the wrong direction. Jeff cared about me and began to make me a little uncomfortable. He told me that my focus should be more on loving God daily than on hitting on the freshman girls. He introduced me to a lot of Christian music that touched my heart and some great Christian books that I had never heard of before. He would ask me why I didn't have a daily devotional. Basically, God used him to convict me in a very good way. Oddly enough, I have never been afraid to be convicted. I have always been more nervous about not feeling conviction over sin and disobedience to Christ. God was working in my life.

Several weeks into my first semester at OBU, the college ministry put on a campus revival. There were several events that preceded the first revival service for the week. One was called Vespers. Vespers was a simple worship service that ended with a short message. The text was Luke 9:23, which says, **"If any man would come after me, He must take up his cross, deny himself daily, and come follow me."** I don't remember who the speaker was, but I was moved. I contemplated the idea and quickly went back to my dorm room.

The next morning was Sunday morning, and I went to church with some friends. The sermon that morning was on Luke 9:23. All day long a battle was raging in my heart. I decided to go to an evening service at another church across town. The text of the message was Luke 9:23. But my heart had been so hardened by my disobedience to

God that I just wasn't getting the message. I was choosing to be stubborn.

On Monday night, the campus revival began, with Dr. Jimmy Draper as the keynote speaker. I'm sure you can guess what the text of his sermon was. Luke 9:23! How much more could a guy take? During the closing of Dr. Draper's sermon, my heart started to break and tears blurred my vision. I loved Jesus, and I knew that He loved me. I had been living a life where I was the center, and I had no real joy or peace. Insecurity weighed me down. I wanted Christ to consume me.

As I walked back from Yarborough Auditorium, I couldn't stop thinking about Luke 9:23. If I really wanted to follow Jesus, I had to be willing to die to my own lordship and my own self-worship. I remember walking through the lobby of Brotherhood Dorm and falling on my knees with Jeff Coleman at my side. In that moment, I surrendered all of my future, all of my talents, and all of my fears and weaknesses to Christ. It was a defining moment in my life.

Don't get me wrong, I didn't enter into a state of perfect bliss, but I did understand what Christ wanted of me—the "cost of discipleship." Also, I began to experience the presence of Christ in a way that I never had before. I remember going into a study room in my dorm, turning the lights off, and praying for over two hours. During that time, it was almost like I heard God's audible voice telling me that he was going to give me a national ministry. I felt such joy and at the same time a deep burden to see my campus and the world take Christ more seriously. God's manifest presence was so palpable that I almost thought heaven had invaded my study room! I still had major hang-ups, but God was more real to me than ever before.

Each day I would carve out time to spend with Christ. My desires and motives began to change.

The next summer I auditioned for a cheesy traveling singing group and made it. I was to sing at the place where I took my first step towards Christ, Falls Creek. In seven weeks, I was going to sing in front of 36,000 students. Our group prepared for a month while living at the Baptist Mission Center in downtown Oklahoma City. During the mornings and evenings, we would minister to the hurting and poverty-stricken kids around the area. We rehearsed in the afternoons. It was truly a life-changing summer because I learned what real ministry looked like. Real ministry is not just standing on a stage in front of 5000 people. Authentic Christianity is a lifestyle and is best manifested in personal relationships.

We played basketball with kids from the "hood"—white, black, Hispanic, and Native American kids who knew the tough side of life. I remember being in a Bible study one night when rival gang members jumped out of a car with baseball bats. Some gang kids were participating in our study and were on the wrong turf. For some crazy reason, I jumped up from the grass in front of the leader and begged them to leave "in the name of Jesus." They left! Another time, the Lord woke me up in the middle of the night. I had a feeling that someone had broken in downstairs. I went downstairs to see what was going on, and suddenly a big Hispanic kid pulls out a knife! Being the true minister that I was, I pulled out a Christian flag pole with a pointy end and thrust it right at him. I yelled, and the guy decided to leave (praise God).

The kind of Christianity that you and I are most familiar with is the kind that is safe and easy. But true Christianity is raw and can be dangerous. I saw what real Christianity looked like that summer, and I wanted more.

My next year in school was great. I considered myself to be the mature college sophomore. One day, in the beginning of the fall semester, I gave some new students a tour around the campus. The next day, some guy walked into my room, and I had no idea who he was.

"Engle, you and I are going to be best friends," he said to me.

I was very quiet, smiling politely as I sarcastically thought, "Sure we are. I *want* to be best friends with a psychopath."

His name was Thomas Young, and he had been in the group from the day before. He told me he saw Jesus Christ in my life, and he shared how only six months earlier he had been an alcoholic on the verge of suicide. Christ had come into his life, and now he sensed the call to preach the gospel. Thomas and I became best friends for over 20 years. God gave us each other because we really had no one else who understood our struggles. We adopted each other as "blood brothers" and challenged, supported, and grew in ministry and in life together. Not too long ago, Thomas passed away and a part of me died too. He is in heaven, and I will see him again.

I used to love rollercoaster rides—my wife still does. I loved them until I developed a knack for motion sickness sometime in college. Now I just become abnormally sick and nauseous on the rides—I avoid them like the plague. The Christian life can be like a rollercoaster. One minute we feel the presence of God and it is so real, and the next day we follow our fleshly instincts like the meeting with God never even happened. When we take our eyes off of Christ and put them on ourselves, we wind up with spiritual nausea. This world does not agree with who we are in Christ. We lack faith. We don't trust God until the trials come, or until our self-dependence makes us miserable.

I am glad for "do over's" though, aren't you? Is God a golfer? If he is, he doesn't play as a professional, but for recreation. I can say this with confidence because God practically invented the mulligan. God is constantly giving us mulligans in life. He is a God who gives us another chance and then another—even when we don't deserve it.

Psalm 86:15 "But You, Lord, are a compassionate and gracious God, slow to anger and abundant in faithful love and truth."

15

DON JUAN DOESN'T KNOW HOW TO LOVE

The story of Don Juan is foreign to me. I have never read a book or a story about the famous conqueror of women. I rented a really sappy Johnny Depp movie that was supposed to be about the guy, but I fell asleep within the first hour of the DVD. I guess there weren't enough explosions. Anyway, Don Juan is supposed to be the greatest lover of all time, but I seriously doubt it. I think Don Juan probably had a hole in his heart the size of Wyoming. True love comes from God.

I saw Valerie for the first time as I was walking into Lara Scales cafeteria for dinner. I had always hated it when people would say to me, "You will just know when you meet the girl you are going to marry." People can just drive you crazy with simplistic notions of romance that leap-frog reality. However, it can *really* drive you crazy when those simplistic notions are right! The second that I saw her golden hair and her sophisticated smile, I knew that Valerie was going to be the girl I would marry. Don't get mad at me for saying that; I hate not being original, and I know it seems like a really bad John Cusak movie—but it actually happened that way.

I am not going to say much about her boyfriend at the time. He was the embodiment of everything that I disliked in humanity. Good-looking and well-dressed with an athletic build, I knew he was a loser from the start. He had to go.

I waited for them to break up, and just as I had anticipated, I received the news a few months later that Valerie had told him to take a hike. I knew she was smart. However, by the time they broke up, I had started dating another girl! I guess I wasn't so smart. I know, I had no faith, I wasn't true to love and all of that, but it is hard for a guy to resist beautiful hair. While I was waiting for Valerie to break up with Mr. Perfect, I met Beautiful Hair Girl. She was a really sweet girl from Arizona, but it wasn't meant to last.

In the spring of my junior year in college, I decided to make my move on Valerie. I saw her in Lara Scales during lunch time, sitting with a group of mutual friends. As I sat down with my scrumptious cafeteria food, I could hear Valerie's conversation. Not only could this gorgeous specimen of the female gender talk, but she was profoundly intelligent. I listened giddily as she waxed eloquent on politics, social reform, and . . . other stuff that I didn't quite understand. But that wasn't important. The important thing was that *she* understood what she was talking about! I was definitely in love. As I stared into her slightly freckled, elegant face, my artificial tapioca pudding actually tasted good. At that moment I never wanted lunch to end. I think romance makes dorks out of us all.

I thought of myself as a highly recognizable upper classman at OBU. In my mind, I was a high-profile kind of guy. I was the first student to ever open up for a major Christian artist, and there weren't a whole lot of events at OBU that I didn't sing at, so Valerie certainly had to know who I was. I was JOEL ENGLE!!!!!

The next day, I happened to see Valerie passing by in the Student Center. I can remember saying to her, "Hey Valerie" as I stopped, smiled, and waited for her to melt at my mere presence.

One of the things that I have always loved about Valerie is her innocent honesty. She is a completely honest person, but in a really nice way. You can imagine my horror as Valerie didn't stop to recognize me. Instead, she walked past me a few feet before turning around and saying, "I'm sorry, have we met?"

"Have we met?" I thought to myself incredulously. I quickly gathered my wits and responded, "Oh . . . um . . . well . . . we . . . um . . . had lunch . . . you know . . . um . . . yesterday . . . Joel Engle . . . my name is Joel Engle . . . haven't you heard me si- . . . Joel Engle . . . I gotta go . . . bye." She stared at me awkwardly, and I pivoted military-style to sprint to the door as fast as I could.

I finally got enough nerve to ask Valerie out on a date. We started going out and became great friends. The reason we became great friends was because that is all Valerie wanted out of our relationship. However, we began to get serious after a few months of getting to know each other.

Valerie is a very different person than I am. She enjoys being alone, she works to relax, and she is almost always kind to people—even me. Although she is a highly intelligent person, she is surprisingly simple in nature. Her upbringing was basically normal. Her mom was a true homemaker and was high-energy all the way. Her dad, Bill, was a successful salesman. He and I had very similar personalities. Bill never met a stranger, and neither have I. Valerie never experimented with partying and enjoyed living in the same place most of her life. She grew up on a golf course, but she never played golf, which is a tragedy.

Although Valerie and I came from much different backgrounds, we had a bond at the heart. Valerie is a great listener, and I needed someone to listen to me. I had never really shared all of my hurt and heartache with anyone except Thomas. Thomas had his own problems to deal with, so we kind of suffered together. I rarely allowed myself to dwell on thoughts of self-pity because I thought that was weak and un-Christian. Yet, slowly, I began to allow Valerie to enter into my secret life of pain. Up to that point in my life, I had bottled up my anger and suffering, except for some fights with other guys or an occasional outburst. Mostly though, I lived on an island by myself. Until I met Valerie.

Valerie and I had been dating for about six months or so, and our relationship was growing with intensity each day. My good friend Bobby had just lost his father to suicide, and I was going to support him and his family during this dismal episode of their lives. I had met Bobby earlier that summer, and when he came to OBU that fall, I began to disciple him. Nobody saw his dad's suicide coming. I decided to travel to the small town of Westville, Oklahoma to support Bobby and his family, and Valerie came with me.

On our way to Westville, we went through the small town of Okmulgee, Oklahoma. I stopped my car at one of the sole traffic lights in the town, and seemingly out of nowhere something exploded inside of me. I am not sure what triggered the eruption of emotion, but it was fierce. As I waited in the car for the light to change green, an anger that I had never felt before heated to the boiling point. For no comprehensible reason, I grabbed the huge glass of water in the cup-holder and threw it against the windshield. The cup detonated, and all of its contents splashed throughout the car. Every curse word you could imagine came out of my mouth. I screamed at Valerie and began to pound the steering wheel as hard as I could, crying in rage. That was the day the pain of my life caught up with me.

I had been living in survival mode since the day I found Mom in the kitchen. When a child is traumatized, he subconsciously builds a wall of protection around his heart. Just like New Orleans that fateful August, the levee of my heart couldn't stand the pressure of the pain pushing against it. Soon, anger turned to sorrow. How could I be a real Christian and have that kind of anger inside of me? It was a violent anger. This was the first of many subconscious tests that I would make Valerie take to see if she really loved me and would stay with me. It is a vicious cycle when you test people's love; they can never pass the test until the cycle is broken. Usually, the cycle never gets broken and the relationship either ends in divorce or separation. That's why many marriages don't survive.

It would take many years for me to be able to trust God enough to walk in the power of His love, so that this pattern of "rejecting love" could be broken.

Understand this: I never, ever wanted to hurt Valerie. It is flat-out wrong for a person to behave that way. The sad thing is that I loved her so much, and she loved me as well. God fused our souls together, and that union was being attacked by my insecurity and unresolved pain. Soon, I would run away from Valerie and we would break up several times. Fear was chasing me again. I hate that I am the person who has hurt her deepest.

Now I have experienced the power of forgiveness from my devoted Heavenly Father who will never leave me or forsake me. Standing in my own merit, I know that I have never deserved forgiveness for the things that I have done. I have also seen forgiveness demonstrated many times in the human realm through Valerie. She has loved me through the darkest days of my life and through my terrible weakness and wounds of the past—despite painful words I have spoken. Her experience of God's love allowed her to love me.

That is how it works. Until you experience the enchanting and healing love of God the Father, through Jesus Christ, you will never be able to extend that love to others. If God is love, then we need Him to be able to love, because real love can only come from Him. I had heard about this love in church, but it never connected to my life. Mostly what I learned from church was to try and be a good person and how to feel guilty for not telling people about Jesus. The problem was that I told a lot of people about Jesus, but I couldn't seem to be good. At least not on the inside. What I missed is that the Christian life is not about behavior modification, but a passionate love affair with Jesus Christ, the real person. Much of my Christian life was motivated by fear. Even though I had a defining moment with God earlier, I had not dealt with the intense fear I had of being abandoned. That is one of the reasons that I couldn't seem to get my belief system and my behavioral system to function at the same time. But that was about to change when God showed me his love in such a way that I could never be the same again.

1 John 4:18-19 "There is no fear in love; instead, perfect love drives out fear, because fear involves punishment. So the one who fears has not reached perfection in love. We love because He first loved us."

16

REALITY AND THE LONE RANGER

L ife is not like a TV show. There are no tight, 20 minute storylines that we follow between commercial breaks. Happy endings are rare. Life is a journey through pain, suffering, occasional highs, and consistent struggles.

When I was a kid, I would watch the Lone Ranger. He had a mask and rode a horse named Trigger. Now that I look back on it, he wasn't that cool, but I thought he was awesome back in the day. He didn't really need anybody; he just shot the bad guys and rode away. Every once in awhile his buddy Tonto would try to help him out, but usually Tonto would just get into trouble. This gave the Lone Ranger yet another excuse to shoot the bad guys, free Tonto from their clutches, and ride away. No matter how dire a situation looked in the middle of the show, everything always worked out perfectly by the end. I thought that it would be a good way to live, minus the shooting people. But life doesn't work like TV.

Valerie and I were engaged at the end of my senior year at OBU. The day I graduated from college was the day that I realized I had no idea what I was going to do with my life. I panicked. Everybody was telling me that I would be stupid not to marry Valerie, and some even mentioned that if I didn't, she would be taken away from me by someone who could appreciate her more. Most people were joking about the last part, but I allowed it to soak into the place of my deepest fears. Valerie was the first person I truly opened up to—the first I ever let inside. She was my dream girl. Remember that cheesy 80's movie "Weird Science?" Two computer nerds in high school write a software program that is supposed to create the perfect woman. Well, to me, Valerie was the perfect girl—too perfect. How could someone as smart, centered, beautiful, and genuine love someone so foolish, broken, and unattractive as me? I was tired of being the Lone Ranger, but I was too scared to change channels. I couldn't believe that Valerie forgave me for the blow up in the car and the many other episodes of my anger and insecurity.

All of the outside pressure to "not lose" Valerie and the internal pressure to marry her before she "got away" convinced me to propose to her. To my total shock and surprise, she said "yes." This was the beginning of the deterioration of our relationship.

With the engagement came the pressure of trying to figure out how I was going to provide for Valerie. It was just too much, and it pushed me over the edge. At this stage in American history the phrase "panic attack" was not a standard part of our vocabulary. Yet I was experiencing very real "panic attacks," to the point where I thought I was literally having a cardiac arrest. In the middle of the night I would wake up in sheer terror and drenched in sweat. My stomach was irritable all the time, and I stopped eating. I went to an ER one night, and they ran me through a series of tests. The diagnosis was that my symptoms were all stress related. I wanted out of the pressure of marriage, but I couldn't find the nerve to break it off. I was on the verge of a mental breakdown. Even though I desperately wanted Valerie in my life, I couldn't stop being the Lone

Ranger. I broke our engagement off a few months before the wedding, and in doing so I broke the heart of the only girl I ever really loved. She didn't understand, and neither did my friends. I felt like a social pariah—lost and alone. I didn't know why the overwhelming emotions were destroying my life, so I ran.

After graduation, I spent the summer traveling around Oklahoma, leading worship. I was staying with my brother and his new wife Krystal as I tried to decide what to do with my life. I had an opportunity to get my master's degree in Chicago and was seriously contemplating the move, but something was not right. As I was driving home from an event in Arkansas, my buddy and I spent the night with some friends of his who lived in Poteau, Oklahoma. I remember thinking that Poteau sounded dangerously close to "Podunk."

Spending the night in strange rooms was nothing new for me—I was a traveling musician. But that night was out of the ordinary. In the stillness of the room, surrounded by someone else's belongings, I heard a voice. It was not audible to human ear but every bit as clear. In that moment I had nowhere to turn, no idea what to do with my life, and from the midst of that tangle of doubt and fear deep inside of me, a voice spoke. "I want you to move to Poteau!"

Poteau, Oklahoma is a small, tree-laden town with the world's smallest mountain (or largest hill) in Eastern Oklahoma. It was the last place on the planet that I wanted to move except for the fact that God made it quite clear that it was the place where I was to live.

You have to understand that at this point in my journey with God and ministry I was "burned out" and disillusioned. Valerie and I were no more, I had no job or any plan, and I was deeply hurt and alone. I had been hurt by religion and by the emptiness of the many "dead" churches that I had been singing in through my music ministry. I was seriously considering leaving the ministry when I met Dan Fisher.

Dan Fisher is an amazing guy. He looks like a young Gene Hackman, is an intellectual genius, has a biting sense of humor, and longed to see real Christianity the way that I did. He was the pastor of a small but growing church in town, and he and I met for the first time at the Black Angus Café. It was the "fancy" restaurant in Poteau. As we met, I shared my hurt and frustration in ministry and in life with him. He just listened and encouraged me. A few days later Dan asked if I would play some of my songs for him. I played them for him, and he looked at me and said in his gravely voice "Wow, man! You have got it!"

He had no idea how bad I needed to hear that. Dan and his wife Pam took me in and basically adopted me. As I struggled with my life, the Fishers were there for me. Dan spent massive amounts of time with me and I would listen to his preaching tapes at night. My apartment was transformed into a small, stinky version of seminary. Dan taught me the how to love the Bible. He also taught me how important friendship is because he gave it to me free of charge. He broke into my personal life and challenged me, sometimes "letting me have it" for my own good.

One thing I loved about Dan was that he wasn't afraid to be a human being who struggled with patience. I remember when Dan and Pam built a new house about four miles outside of Poteau. We were moving some furniture from their apartment to the new house, and as we drove up the gravel road to their house, it began to rain. The stuff in the back of the truck was uncovered and getting soaked. The construction guys were driving right at us and Pam was in a car behind us, so we were sandwiched with nowhere to go! The expression on Dan's face and the flurry of frustrated humor that came out of his mouth was priceless. We finally got up to the house and began to remove the huge entertainment center from the back of Dan's truck. As we picked it up, all of the ball-bearings inside the door fell out and the entertainment center fell apart all over the truck! Dan just looked at me and Pam and we all laughed until we cried. Those were good days living out life together.

Christianity is supposed to be communal. As much as we need to experience the presence of Christ in our individual lives, we need each other just as badly. True Christianity is not about going to a church service to hear some Bible teaching and a good praise band, it is about sharing life together. I can honestly say that my time in Poteau with Dan and Pam was one of the sweetest times in my life because I saw the possibilities of what Christianity could be with other people.

After about a year, I moved to Oklahoma City to take a position at a large church as an associate student pastor. It was an extremely difficult decision, and Dan was really against it. When I look back at that decision, I think my fear of being known and rejected was so strong that I couldn't stay in a place where that was a possibility. It was a very bad move for me, and once again I almost quit the ministry. The church that I served in was about as dysfunctional as an episode of Jersey Shore. It was human.

As God would have it, Dan and Pam moved from Poteau about a year later. Dan became the pastor of a church in Yukon, Oklahoma, just outside of OKC. I was excited when Dan told me that they would be moving within 30 minutes of where I lived. I soon left my position at the church I was working for and joined them at Yukon. I quickly became involved with Dan and Pam's ministry at Trinity Church.

It was during this time that Valerie and I reconnected. Although we both wanted to move forward in our relationship, there were still walls to tear down and roadblocks to remove. Our relationship at that time can best be described as "off and on." Dan told me that I needed to deal with my issues in my relationship with Valerie and stop running. He was probably right, but in my heart of hearts I didn't feel that I had established my music ministry enough to provide for her. Moreover, I still had a deep fear of getting married.

Despite all of that messiness, I loved her. All I could do was think about her and want to talk to her. One month, my phone bill was over $300! It was worth it. But I was still afraid because I didn't want to get into another situation with Valerie where my anger, pain, and idiosyncrasies could destroy her. Plus, there was the conflict of my growing music ministry. All I ever really wanted to do in life was write songs and sing about the greatness of Jesus Christ. I knew in my heart that this was my true calling, but many "wise" people told me to get a "day-job." The problem was that if you have the talent to do music for a living, you must be totally and completely dedicated to it. That meant doing whatever it took to make music my "real job." This was my opportunity to use music and ministry as my cover story so I could run. Many people run into ministry to hide from their junk, and I was no different.

The Lone Ranger rides again.

17

NOT-SO-GREAT EXPECTATIONS

Currently, I am the pastor of The Exchange Church in Keller, Texas. I honestly can't believe that I am a pastor. Aside from Dan Fisher, I pretty much thought pastors were dorks. I had this picture in my mind of a guy with a bad comb-over wearing a sports jacket and tie, saying "Amen" way too much. God has a sense of humor—that is for sure. The Exchange Church is a church that I started from scratch with some friends a few years ago. When I started telling people that I was leaving Christian music to plant a church, some of them said to me "Joel, you don't know what you are getting into planting a church. It is extremely difficult work."

My response was, "Have you ever started a traveling music ministry in 1987 with only a keyboard? Now *that* is hard work."

Then I would receive the look. You know—"the look."

Making it as a traveling Christian musician is extremely difficult. It involves sacrifice. Normal things that people do like going to movies, hunting trips, Bible studies, Sunday morning services, and so forth are hard because of the intense travel schedule. I would be gone for weeks—even months—at a time, and I would arrive home incredibly tired and weirded-out because I didn't know how to relate to people who had 9-to-5 jobs. They certainly don't know how to relate to me.

I also had to be able to write and record my own music and have a decent talent for marketing. It takes a lot of guts to write and record a song you have written. It also takes a lot of money. I don't know anybody who had more drive to "make it" than I did. It was the looming question in my mind. "Will I be able to fulfill the dream of seeing my message and music become my full-time career?"

I have been blessed by God (not lucky) because I have always made a living doing music. I have never been hugely successful, but I have been greatly blessed to have my music on the radio, to have opportunities to play my songs all over the country, and to have met so many great people along the way. Yet, it is a life of isolation. During the beginning stages of my music ministry/career, I was incredibly lonely. I traveled primarily by myself as a solo artist, and was alienated from my friends because of the solitary nature of my calling.

When I was 23, I "made it" to the big time. A prominent youth speaker's ministry brought me on their national tour. I traveled with them for three years. I met some good people during that time, but it was the low point of my life. I realized that being "big time" was not what it was cracked up to be. I was becoming cynical and arrogant. It was at that moment in my life when I realized that success didn't validate me as a person.

I thought that as soon as I became a well-known Christian musician, I would feel better about myself and about life. I thought that if I could reach my dream of singing my songs in front of thousands of people and seeing their lives changed, I would be happy. Then I experienced my goal and saw thousands of teenagers come to know Christ, but I was still struggling with despair. My expectations were not met because the very premises of my hopes were radically distorted. I realized that just because I was successful in ministry didn't mean that I was automatically Christ-like.

In my mind I had fostered the expectation that when I "made it" with my music ministry, I would be surrounded by godly men who would take me under their wings and disciple me. Instead, most of what was modeled for me during that period of my life was what I didn't want to be. I was amazed that the "Christian" leaders in the organization weren't always perfect. They were even dysfunctional (just like me) and did things that hurt me deeply. God had given me exactly what I wanted, but I discovered that it wasn't fulfilling. What I truly wanted was purpose and peace.

The ironic thing was that when I was in Poteau and Yukon struggling with "making it," I was happy because I was dependent on the Lord and encircled by people who I trusted and loved. I thought that "making it" with my music was what I needed. Yet it was really Jesus that my heart was longing for: I just didn't understand it yet.

During that time, Valerie and I decided to get married. After a few miserable relationships with girls on the road, I realized that Valerie was the girl for me. Todd and Al were a part of the ministry that I was involved with, and they (like just about everybody else) really encouraged me to deal with my junk and get back with Valerie. I told Todd how much I missed her, and he gave me some great advice. With Todd's encouragement, I began to write to Valerie every day. I didn't send her e-mails or texts, but wrote letters sent snail mail/old school style. Finally, Valerie and I started dating again. Within a few weeks I knew beyond the shadow of a doubt that we were supposed to be married. The problem was that I had no idea how to ask for her hand because this was our third engagement! Todd, being the romantic genius that he was, helped me figure out how to propose to Valerie. Valerie worked in Oklahoma City at a doctor's office. I had some friends show up at her job (with her boss' permission) and kidnap her by driving her to the airport. She got on the next flight to Dallas where I picked her up. She was still in her all-white nurse's outfit as I drove her to Todd and Lisa's (Todd's wife) house. I had purchased a new dress, shoes, and accessories for her to wear, and she changed and I took her out to a very expensive French restaurant where we sat and smiled at each other for an hour. We went for a walk after dinner, and my friend Al had set up a table for two on the grass next to the riverwalk. It was there that I got down on my knee and asked her to marry me! She said "yes" again, and 3 months later we were hitched!

Valerie jumped with me into the middle of the chaos of traveling over 280 days a year on the road. No wonder we had such enormous problems in our relationship; a human being is not created to be in transit that many times a year. I was stressed out and so was she. During those three years with the traveling ministry, I had become somewhat famous. Well, for the tiny American Christian sub-culture, I was slightly famous. My identity in the church had been carved out, and I routinely sang in front crowds of over 3000-10000 people. I was starting to get recognized in airports and at malls. But at the pinnacle of what I once thought were my wildest dreams, the toll of traveling and some personality conflicts let me resign from the ministry I was working with. I decided to venture out on my own. I had convinced myself that when I left the ministry, all of the major record labels would come running to my door to sign me to a contract. I was just replacing old expectations with new ones. Instead of a major label frenzy of men in suits holding contracts, all that I heard where the empty sounds of crickets chirping in the hollow background of my failed existence.

My calendar had come to a screeching halt, and I had to deal with who I really was as a person and how I was going to provide for Valerie. That was difficult—painfully difficult—because I felt like a nobody. I felt that God had left me alone to rot in my self-pity. Yet, it was in this quiet time in the wilderness when God seemed to force me to slow down and take inventory. I couldn't run anymore. It was like being introduced to someone you instantly feel an aversion toward—only I was being introduced to myself. What was so cool was that God was bringing me to the end of myself.

One of my life passages in the Bible is 2 Corinthians 2:8-9. Paul was going through a terrible time in his life where it seemed that his ministry was permanently coming to an end and that he might even be killed because of loving Christ.

> **2 Corinthians 1:8-9** "We do not want you to be uninformed, brothers, about the hardships we suffered in the province of Asia. We were under great pressure, far beyond our ability to endure, so that we despaired even of life. Indeed, in our hearts we felt the sentence of death. But this happened that we might not rely on ourselves but on God, who raises the dead.

God, in His great love for me, let me come to the end of myself. Why? So that through the pain of the emptiness of human existence, I would stop depending on my survival instincts and natural talent and start depending upon His supernatural life in me. This process was started when my expectations came crashing to the ground at about the speed of light. When the dust settled, my plastic dreams where burnt up and replaced by the infinite love of the God of the heavens and the earth. When my puny, self-centered expectations were destroyed, hope exploded into my heart. The show was over, but the story was just beginning.

18

ALGEBRAPHOBIA

When I was in second grade, I had a babysitter who was a ninth grader named Cindy Lietzke. She was beautiful; naturally, I was madly in love with her. She had beautifully long, brown hair and was so nice to me. However, Cindy scarred me for life.

One day Cindy told me "Joel, when you get to ninth grade, you are going to have to take the most terrible and incredibly hard class in the world. It's called Algebra and it will kill you."

This was not good news for a second grader who already hated math. After Cindy's statement, I contracted what I call "algebraphobia" and dreaded every year that nudged me toward that horrific and demonic math course.

The years went by, and each year I dreaded the fact that Algebra was closing in on me. Then one August morning in the beginning of ninth grade, I sat in Mr. Tooley's Algebra class. I was paralyzed with distress at my unfortunate situation. Mr. Tooley began to draw a series of numbers on the board. What made it so hideous was that he added "letters" to the numbers. Algebra was alphanumeric: in other words, pure evil. Soon the class was gloriously over, and we were given our homework assignment. I knew that all of my prospects of future employment were dwindling at light speed.

I arrived home and began to look through our textbook for the class. I turned the ominous pages and saw the growing complexity and difficulty mushrooming into a mathematic nuclear explosion for my academic annihilation, but something happened when I got to the end of the book. The publisher of the textbook made a radical and glorious mistake: they put the answers to all of the Algebra equations in the back of the book. How could people who were supposed to be so smart be so joyfully stupid? I was dancing around in my room with euphoria at knowing that not only would I pass Algebra, but that I would now make guaranteed A's in all of my homework assignments. I did my "homework" in about 8 minutes flat and went outside to shoot some baskets.

I remember going to Algebra class two days later with total confidence that I would make the best grade in the class on my homework. How could it be my fault that the trusted brains of the math world were dull-witted enough to put the answers in the back of the book? Mr. Tooley walked around the class, handing out our graded papers as I sat trying to compress the rising joy within my soul. Then I received my graded paper. It was covered in red. On the very top of the page was my "grade" written in wretched red ink. It was a "3." Trust me, a "3" is more humiliating than a zero!

You see, Algebra is all about doing the equations correctly, not just getting the answers right. This was the same thing that happened in my Christian life for many years. I knew a lot of the answers about life and about God, but I didn't know how to work the spiritual equation. For instance, let's take the statement "God loves Joel." I believed that to be a true statement, but the problem was that I had no idea *why* God really loved me. I knew some of the answers, but they didn't register on my emotional radar. For many years, I would sing songs and preach sermons about God's love while at the same time having very little faith that God could really love me because of the emotional anguish and serious sin that I was constantly experiencing. Just like Algebra, I had no clue as to how to do the equation that a holy, righteous, just God could love someone so incapacitated as me. However, God was working in my life and actually tutoring me on how to do the equation of his love and acceptance—and I didn't even know it.

There are two particular watershed moments that helped me learn to do the equation of God's affection for me, which changed my life forever. The first was meeting Louie Giglio. Louie is a well known speaker, author, and all-around brilliant guy. He is the architect for the Passion movement and has influenced Christian music like few people have. We were in Chattanooga, Tennessee doing a conference for youth ministers, and Louie was using Colossians chapter 2 as his text for the three-day event.

One night he asked the question, "How many of you think the Christian life is hard?"

Of course, everybody raised their hands high in the air. Louie responded to their raised hands by saying, "You are wrong. The Christian life is not hard, it is impossible."

Crash!!! You could have heard my theology smash into a thousand pieces on the floor of the auditorium! Over the weekend, Louie explained that Christ was the power source of the Christian life, not our willpower. Of course, I had heard this before, but never with this much understanding and power. That weekend set me on a course to understand the equation of God's love for me.

I asked Louie if there was a book that helped him understand this concept, and he told me about a book called *Lifetime Guarantee* by Dr. Bill Gillham. As soon as I got back home, I bought that book. It was another watershed moment. As I began to read the pages, it was as if the Holy Spirit was shouting into my inner being. For the very first time in my life, the reasons and factual realities of why God loves me were made alive. I learned that I could never do enough to please a holy God by my own efforts. God sent Jesus to die in my place, and Jesus' finished work on the cross is the only thing that makes human beings right with God. Even though I had called upon Christ to be my Lord when I was a teenager, I was reverting back to trying to do things by my own efforts to make God accept me. I realized that Jesus had already met God's standard by living the perfect life no one but He could live, and then by becoming my substitute on the cross, taking God's wrath toward me upon Himself. The realization changed everything for me! On top of all of that, I read a statement that really messed up my world. *"Dear Christian, the Lord never intended you to try your best to live the Christian life. He placed His Spirit within you to love His life through you and to bring glory and honor to Himself. He does His work of ministry on earth through you."*

During those many years of singing, studying the Bible, preaching, and sharing God's love with other people, I was subconsciously trying to earn God's love by doing "stuff" for Him. I would always fail because I could never maintain that high-standard of living. I was trying to please an infinite God by powerless, finite means. I finally realized that Jesus already met God's standard of perfection in His life, death, and resurrection—and He wanted to life His supernatural life through me! The amazing, omnipotent, eternal, and supremely majestic God of the universe was willing (and still is) to live His life through me. I discovered what real Christianity was all about: Christ expressing His life through my life.

Now the Bible reads totally differently than it used to for me. I realize that the subject of the Bible is a loving, redeeming God who wants to empower me with Himself so that I may experience His love, joy, and life. He wants to reveal His abundant life through me to a hurt and dying world.

> Romans 8:11 "And if the Spirit of him who raised Jesus from the dead is living in you, he who raised Christ from the dead will also give life to your mortal bodies through his Spirit, who lives in you."

It is amazing how fun math can be when you know how to do the equations. It is life-transforming when you know that Christ is the equation for our daily living. Maybe math isn't so bad after all.

19

THE FATHER I NEVER HAD

I have something to confess: I have not totally overcome all the problems and trauma of my childhood. I still have pain, and at times I find myself on the emotional roller-coaster of powerfully negative feelings. There is no magical solution to healing damaged emotions. I can tell you that knowing Jesus Christ has radically improved my life, and when I have the faith to depend upon Him, I see a true change in my attitudes and responses. The battle between the flesh and the Spirit rages in my life just like yours, and I hate it just as much as you do.

There are a lot of people who have experienced my ministry over the years who have a high opinion of me because of my testimony, but I would be dishonest if I let my testimony become some kind of heroic legend. If you just listen to the sound bytes of my life, you would come to the conclusion that I have overcome all my problems and am close to perfection.

That couldn't be further from the truth.

I struggle furiously with my flesh, and I long for the day when I will see Christ face-to-face—when the battle will be over. I am not suicidal, just hopeful. Yet, I can also honestly tell you that Christ is enough to give me hope and peace in my life. But in order for me to experience that, I need more than a merely casual relationship with Him. I must totally immerse myself the waves of His grace, mercy, and love. The waves can be huge and frightening, and to dive under them—to let them wash over me—requires faith.

Therein lies the problem: I get lazy and lose faith so quickly. So often I am just like the prodigal son, taking my gifts for granted and feeling like I don't need to work for my Father. But when the Holy Spirit shouts from someplace deep inside of me and I realize my entitlement and laziness, my Father is waiting to accept me back with open arms—and the table is already prepared with a feast.

I was on the road singing with my bandmates at a youth camp when Valerie called me and told me I was going to be a dad. It was one of the most exciting pieces of news I have ever received. So for those nine months preceding our first child's birth, I had one thought on my mind: I am not going to abandon my child like my dad abandoned me.

Walking down the corridor of the hospital, I was trying to remember at least some of the things I had learned in "birthing class." Because of my travel schedule, I actually had "birthing class" in my house. We hired a nurse to teach us how to do whatever it is you are supposed to do during "birthing day." It was weird , and if you ever meet Birthing Nurse Lady, don't let her show you the videos! Valerie and I watched about 4 DVD's that showed different couples going through the birthing process all the way up to the delivery. They showed everything. It was worse than *Nightmare on Elmstreet*!

I really wanted to be a good "coach" to Valerie during her first pregnancy. I don't do much half-heartedly, so in typical Joel fashion, I took the whole "birthing coach" thing very seriously. The problem with all of the classes and "birthing" philosophies is that they don't work on game day. I tried everything they told me, but Valerie's pain was more than we had both expected. All I know is that after 14 hours of hearing Valerie breathe intensely, cry out in pain, and moan and groan, I changed philosophies mid-stream. I became an "epiduralist," and a fanatical one at that. An epidural is a really fancy name for a pain shot, which they put in her lower back. Then, after a few minutes, all of the wailing, shouting, and panicked breathing stopped, and Valerie was as relaxed as a woman in labor could possibly be. I asked for one as well, but the nurse didn't think I needed one as much as Valerie.

We hear the term worship used all the time. Typically it is used to describe a type of music. Yet, my greatest worship experience involved no music whatsoever. It was the day that my daughter Elizabeth was born. I couldn't believe that God would be so good by giving me another chance to have a family of my own. This could be my chance to make up for what was taken away from me. Today, when I look at my children Elizabeth, Evelyn, Elaine, and Ethan, I thank God for the blessing of being their dad. My greatest fear in life is that I will fail them because of my great imperfections. I want to make sure they know that God is a loving Father who they can run to when they are hurting. I don't want them to ever experience pain or suffering, but I know that in this messed up world we live in, they cannot avoid it. Therefore, my job as their father is to teach them how to accept the things that happen that they cannot control, and to fervently trust God—no matter the circumstances.

Elizabeth is a little reflection of myself. She has my little pug nose, my smile, and a large heaping of my personality. She is funny, quick-witted, strong-willed, enthusiastic, and a leader. She is a happy version of how I was as a child.

Evelyn is a lot like her mother. She has big, blue-eyes that sparkle like little marbles. She is incredibly sensitive and has a smile that will melt you.

Elaine is a little bundle of energy. I call her my little "taquito" because she is so small and so cute.

I call Ethan my "little bubsy" after the show Wubsy Wubsy Wow Wow. Don't ask me how that name was derived, and don't ask me to revoke my "man-card" either. I do have to say that it will be great to have a little more testosterone in the house!

The love that I feel inside of my heart for my daughters and son is so strong that it hurts—I would give my life for them in a heartbeat. I think about them all day long, and when a Texas-sized thunderstorm rolls over our town, I worry about them being scared. But I worry about my weaknesses as a man and as a father damaging them more than anything, except maybe the idea of dating. It is just an idea, dating. My daughters will be the first Baptist nuns in the history of the church. They kissed dating goodbye at birth.

It is crazy how being a parent makes you feel so helpless at times. It is because we are not all powerful, all knowing, and all wise. We can't protect our kids from the painful variables of life. We are incomplete in our knowledge of good and therefore wonder if we are doing the right things for our children. We make mistakes because we lack wisdom. That is why we have to turn our children and our lives over to God. God is all-powerful. Nothing can stand against him; He never ever fails and cannot be defeated. God knows our children perfectly. He knows how they are wired on the inside because He is the One who did the electrical work. He never puts anything in their way that is not for their best. His love is absolutely perfect, and He only operates in love towards them.

That is why it is such a big deal to be called a "child of God." Even though I am an earthly father, I am also a son. I have been adopted by the King of the Universe. Just as I have intense concern for my daughters, God has deep care and concern for me, his little boy. My kids do ignorant things because they are not fully developed yet. Evelyn would fall off the bed if I wasn't there to protect her. Elizabeth would run out into a busy street to get her little ball if I wasn't there to stop her. I still do foolish and ignorant things, but I am glad that my heavenly Father is there to stop me.

My girls would eat ice cream for every meal if I let them. I guard what they put into their bodies because I want them to grow up healthily. My Father in heaven guards my spiritual diet and sometimes lets me put things in my life that make me sick. He does this so I will learn that His way is the best way. He is so patient with me.

It kills me when Elizabeth will disobey me or Valerie and we have to discipline her. I hate to make her cry, but sometimes I have to. God has to do the same for us, because He loves us. It is weird that we have to cause pain to show our kids we love them. We don't indulge them because we want them to mature into respectful, kind, and honorable people. God does the same for us. Elizabeth doesn't understand this yet, but she will. I don't know how much I understand God's instruction for me, but I know that it is always what I need.

My life has been a pretty crazy ride up to this point—that is for sure. I know that God is my father; He is the father that I never had on this earth. Sometimes I feel distant to Him, but that is usually my fault, not His. I am learning to trust Him more, and I am beginning to realize that without Him working in my life and living through me, I go right back to square one in my spiritual life. I don't know where you are in your life, but I know this: if you are God's child, He will never leave you or forsake you. He is working in your life and wants to make you more like His Son, Jesus. He is a loving, perfect, and invincible Father who wants to use your life for His glory and purpose.

None of us are perfect people. We have pains, aches of the heart, and hiccups in our personalities. It is hard for us to believe that God could really love us as we are. It is hard to fathom someone totally perfect putting up with someone who is so weak and prone to sin. It is even harder to accept how much we don't really deserve that love. The times in my life when I have accepted God's love have been life-saving moments for me. I never had a dad. I had a grandpa and a few guys down the line who did some fathering for me, but my physical father was never present. I still suffer from of his absence, of that I am sure. Maybe you have a very competent dad who modeled love and integrity for you as a kid. Yet even that dad cannot compare to our heavenly Father. I hope you will spend the rest of your life getting to know your heavenly Father, if you know Him. That truly is the purpose of existence—to know Him and to tell everyone you know how strong, great, and powerful your Heavenly Dad really is. If you don't know Him, then know this: that God willingly sent His Son to come from heaven to Earth to save His chosen ones. He didn't spare any pain, expense, or inconvenience to rescue us from sin. Call out to Him to reveal Himself and His salvation to you. He is our only hope.

Romans 8:32 "He who did not spare his own Son, but gave him up for us all—how will He not also, along with him, graciously give us all things?

LaVergne, TN USA
26 May 2010
184081LV00003B/12/P